MAKING DO IN CHALLENGING TIMES 2020-22

WRITTEN, & ILLUSTRATED BY CAROLYN MACY

PHOTOGRAPHY BY

JEREMY AND CAROLYN MACY

MAKING DO IN CHALLENGING TIMES

2020-22

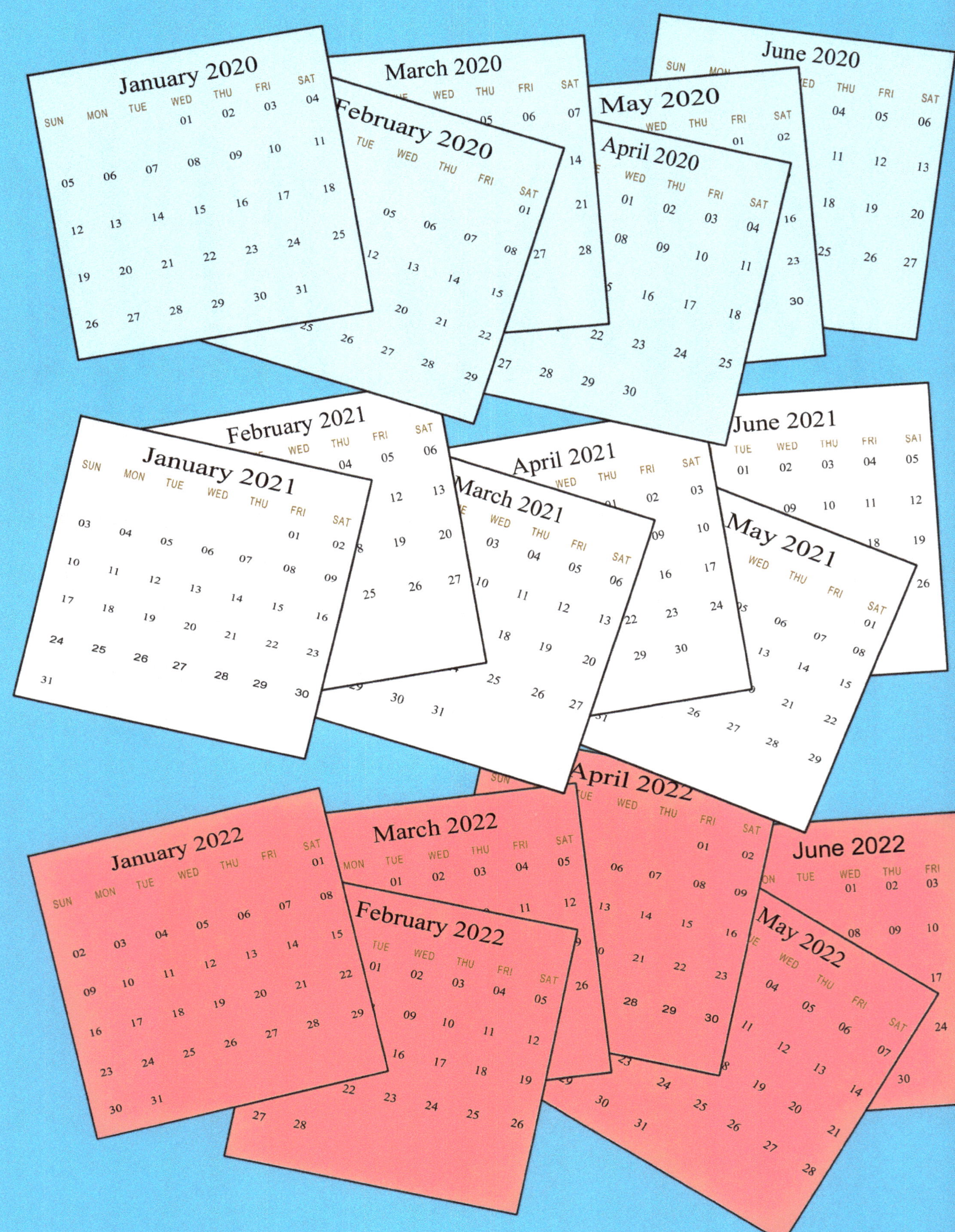

January 2020
SUN MON TUE WED THU FRI SAT
01 02 03 04
05 06 07 08 09 10 11
12 13 14 15 16 17 18
19 20 21 22 23 24 25
26 27 28 29 30 31

February 2020
TUE WED THU FRI SAT
01
05 06 07 08
12 13 14 15
20 21 22
26 27 28 29

March 2020
WED THU FRI SAT
05 06 07

April 2020
WED THU FRI SAT
01 02 03 04
08 09 10 11
16 17 18
22 23 24 25
29 30

May 2020
WED THU FRI SAT
01 02
14
21
16
23 25 26 27
30

June 2020
SUN MON ED THU FRI SAT
04 05 06
11 12 13
18 19 20
25 26 27

January 2021
SUN MON TUE WED THU FRI SAT
01 02
03 04 05 06 07 08 09
10 11 12 13 14 15 16
17 18 19 20 21 22 23
24 25 26 27 28 29 30
31

February 2021
WED THU FRI SAT
04 05 06
12 13
19 20
25 26 27

March 2021
WED THU FRI SAT
03 04 05 06
10 11 12 13
18 19 20
25 26 27
30 31

April 2021
WED THU FRI SAT
01 02 03
09 10
16 17
22 23 24
29 30

May 2021
WED THU FRI SAT
01
05 06 07 08
13 14 15
21 22
28 29

June 2021
TUE WED THU FRI SAI
01 02 03 04 05
09 10 11 12
18 19
26

January 2022
SUN MON TUE WED THU FRI SAT
01
02 03 04 05 06 07 08
09 10 11 12 13 14 15
16 17 18 19 20 21 22
23 24 25 26 27 28 29
30 31

February 2022
TUE WED THU FRI! SAT
01 02 03 04 05
09 10 11 12
16 17 18 19
22 23 24 25 26
27 28

March 2022
MON TUE WED THU FRI SAT
01 02 03 04 05
11 12
20 21 22

April 2022
WED THU FRI SAT
01 02
06 07 08 09
13 14 15 16
21 22 23
28 29 30

May 2022
WED THU FRI SAT
04 05 06 07
11 12 13 14
19 20 21
26 27
28

June 2022
ON TUE WED THU FRI
01 02 03
08 09 10
17
24
30

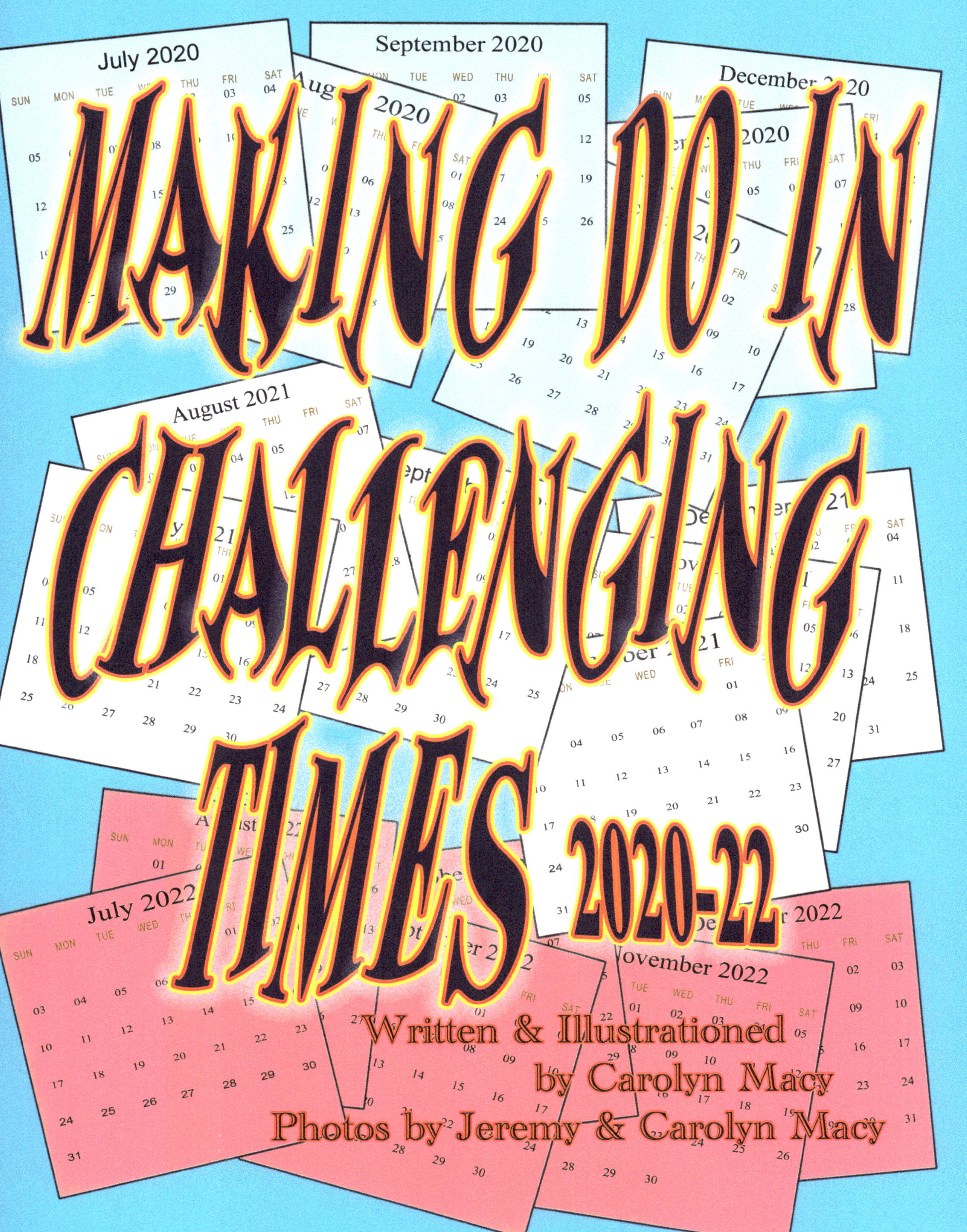
MAKING DO IN CHALLENGING TIMES 2020-22
Written & Illustrationed
by Carolyn Macy
Photos by Jeremy & Carolyn Macy

Dedicated to my
family, and friends.

Making Do In Challenging Times
Copyright©2023 by Carolyn Macy and
Jeremy Macy. All rights reserved.'

Published by Carolyn Macy
6227 81st Ave. N.E. | Norman, Oklahoma 73026 USA
405.401.2012

Book design copyright (c) 2023 by Carolyn Macy.
Written and Illustrated by Carolyn Macy.
Photography by Jeremy and Carolyn Macy.

Published in the United States of America
ISBN: 9781732860476-Softcover
Anthology: Poetry. Photography.

2019

With 2019 ending,
We thought back through the year
Of those eventful moments
We heard or saw appear.

The summertime found us
Where trade wind breezes blow.
We visited our daughter
And many friends we know.

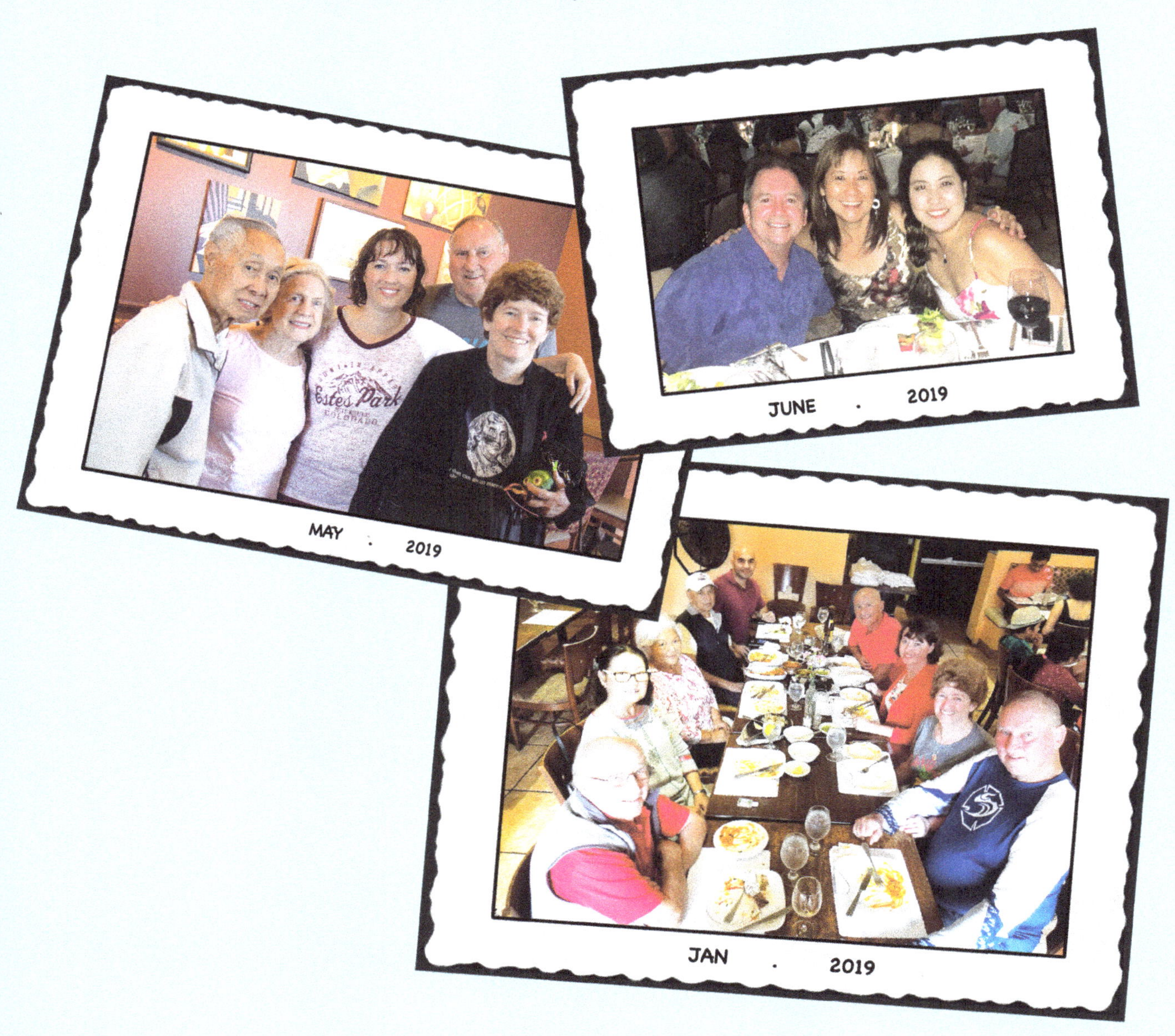

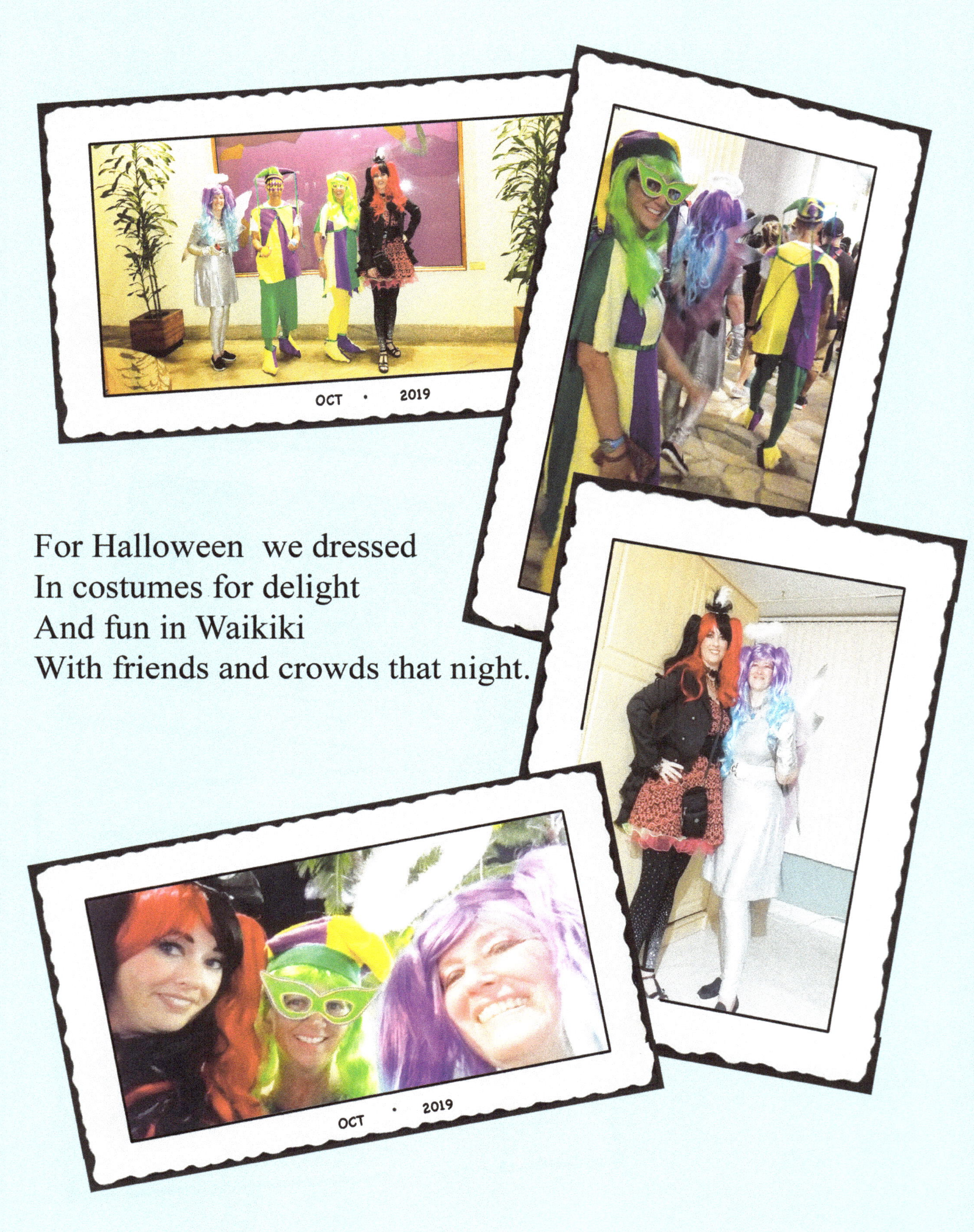

For Halloween we dressed
In costumes for delight
And fun in Waikiki
With friends and crowds that night.

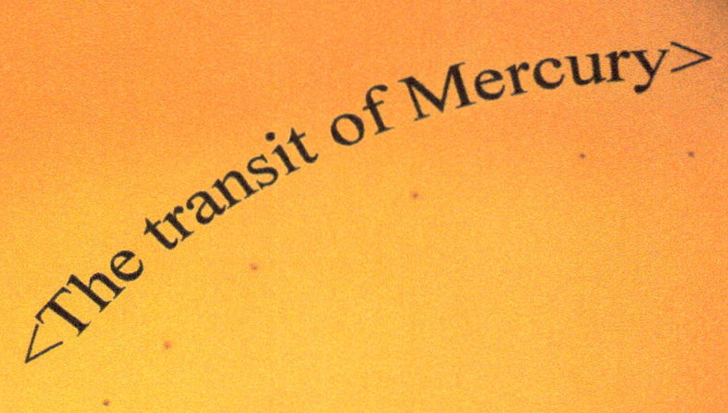

Once home, we drove to catch
The planet Mercury.
It passed before the sun
Which made it plain to see.

NOV . 2019

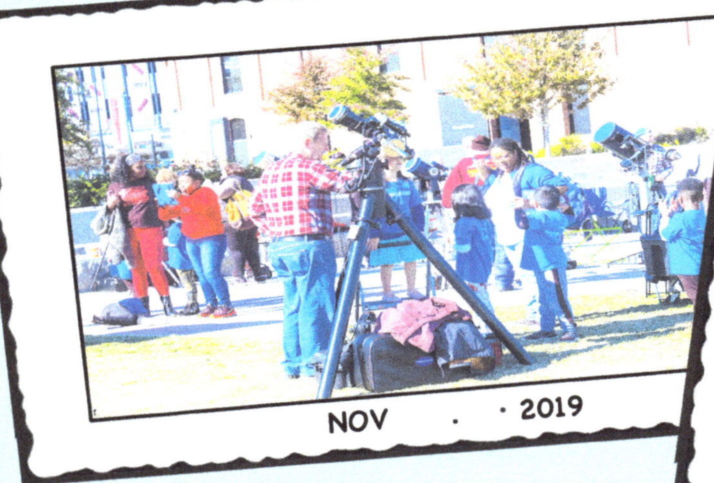
NOV . 2019

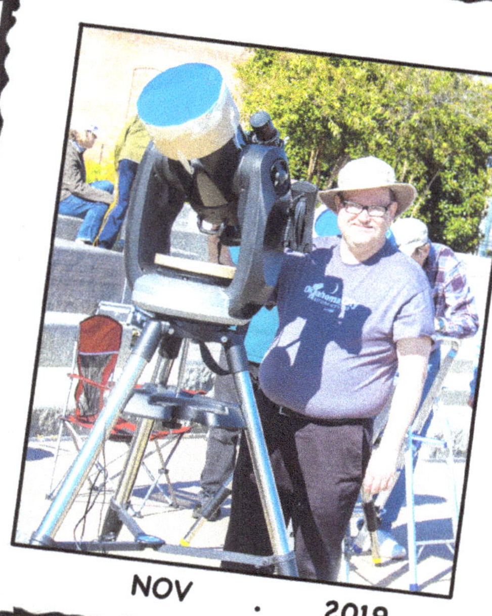
NOV . 2019

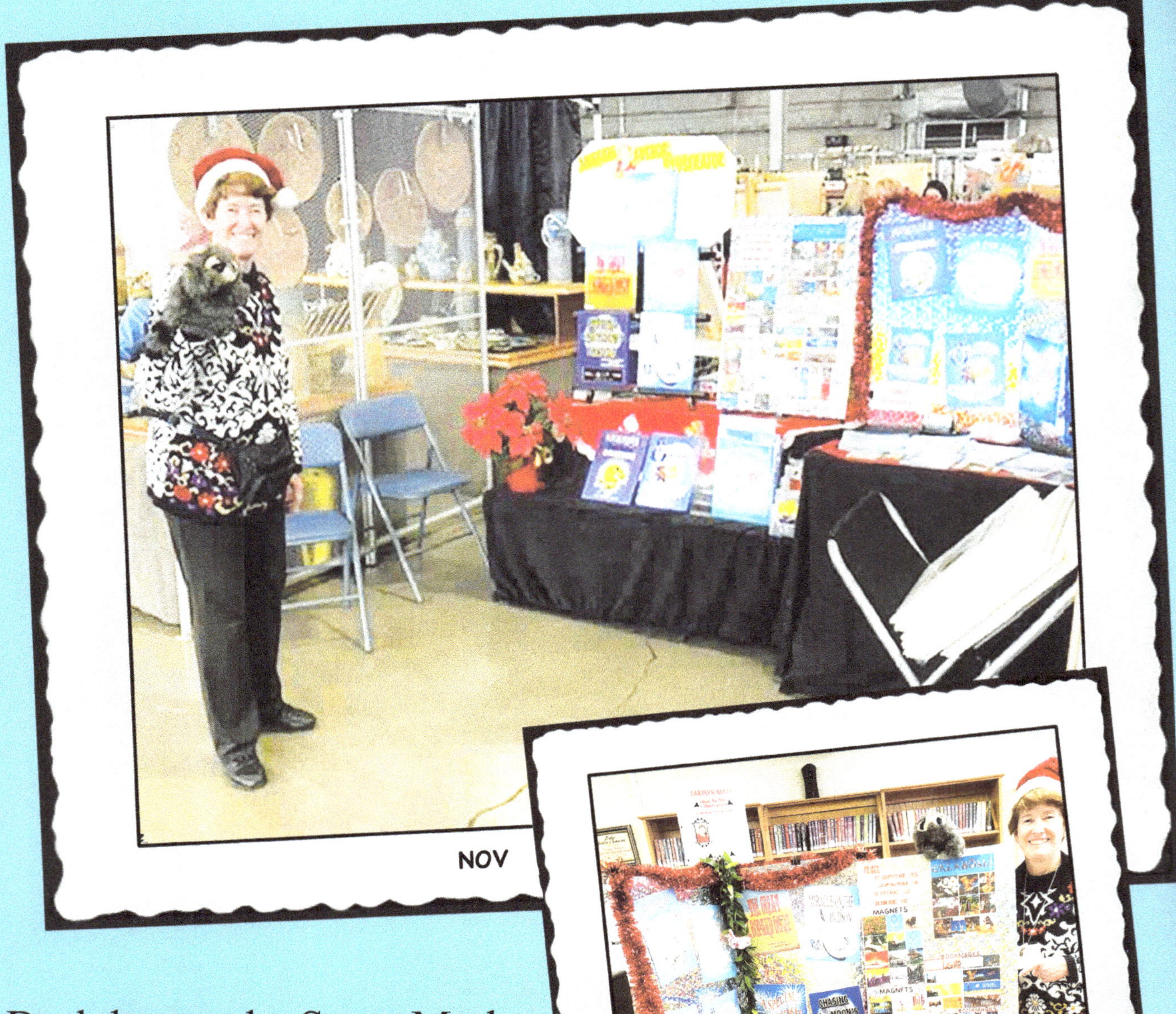

Back home, the Santa Market
Had opened up its door
For vendors selling goods
With much there to explore.

My hometown library
Invited me to come
To hold a book event
And talk about mine some.

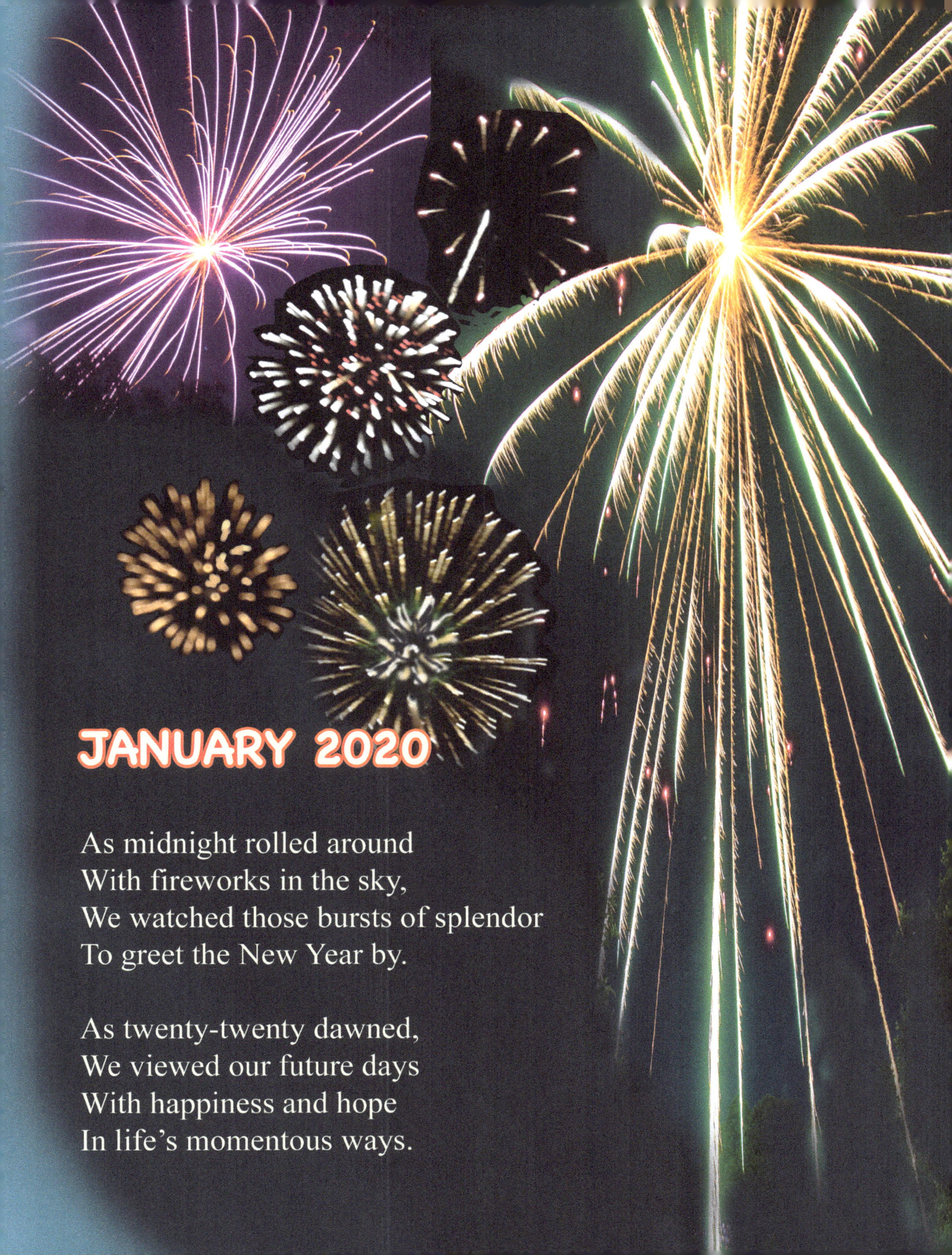

JANUARY 2020

As midnight rolled around
With fireworks in the sky,
We watched those bursts of splendor
To greet the New Year by.

As twenty-twenty dawned,
We viewed our future days
With happiness and hope
In life's momentous ways.

His first impeachment happened
The ending of last year *
As winter days approached
And Christmas time drew near.

No one's above the law,
And breaking it's not right.
He thought he was allowed
And broke it in plain sight.

The House held off until
The Senate made its plan
Just how his trial would run
When once the trial began.

The prosecutors first
Presented in the trial.
New evidence appeared
To come in all the while.

Defenders took their turn.
No witness did they call.
They voted to acquit
In three days overall. *

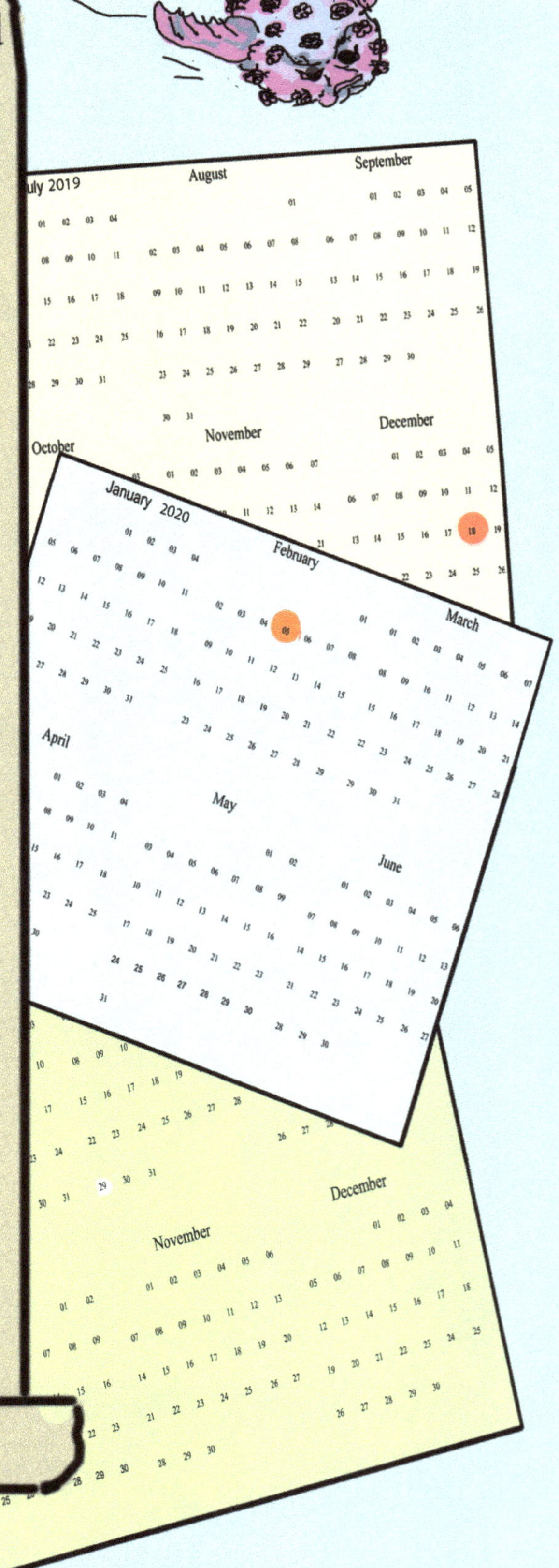

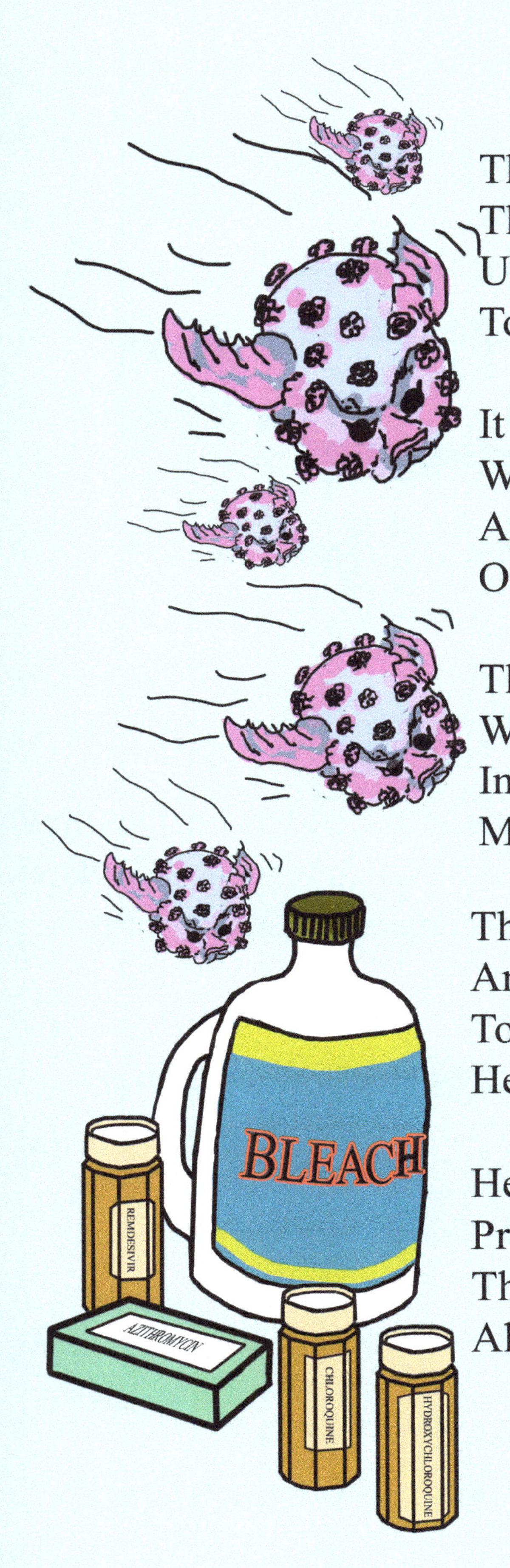

The normal winter days
Then always seemed the same
Until an illness struck
To set the world aflame.

It spread around from China
With such a rapid burst;
Appearing in the state
Of Oregon at first.

The next month came and went
With virus spreading more
In towns and country-sides
Much greater than before.

The White House played it down
And called it, "Just a hoax
To disappear like magic!"
He told the country's folks.

He practiced medicine,
Prescribing cures to take.
The pharmacies and doctors
All warned his cures were fake.

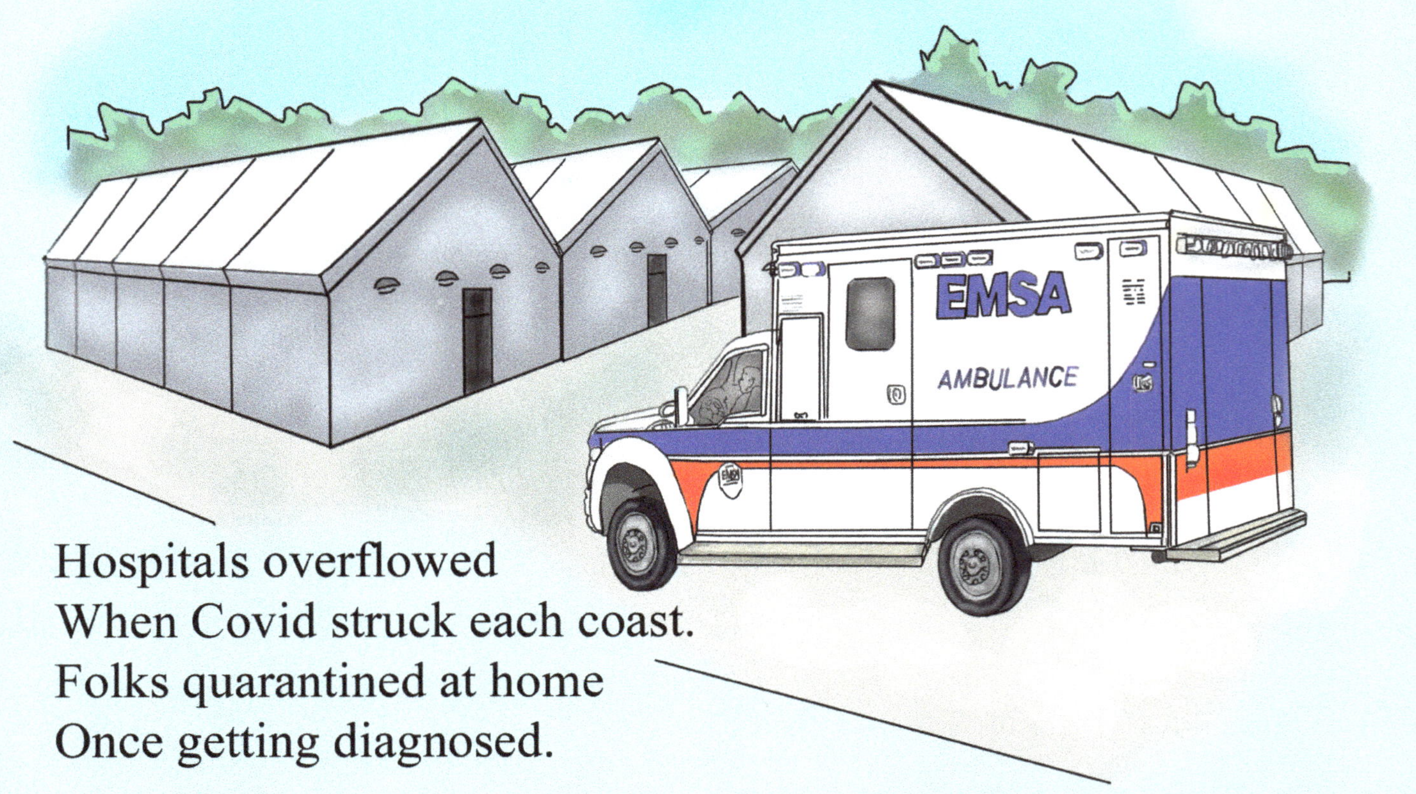

Hospitals overflowed
When Covid struck each coast.
Folks quarantined at home
Once getting diagnosed.

Some folks became so sick,
They sadly passed away,
While others never knew
Their bodies served as prey.

Health workers overwhelmed
At the enormous spreads,
Then called for FEMA's help
For workers, tents, and beds.

Mid-March the virus spread
Had stretched from coast to coast,
Where all along those coastlines
The virus spread the most.

Some cities called for lockdowns
As thousands turned up sick.
They hoped that this might stop
The spread of virus quick.

Then businesses and schools
Shut down and locked their door
To do their work from home
With hopes to slow it more.

In public places folks
Were asked to wear a mask.
Protecting self and others
Proved just too much to ask!

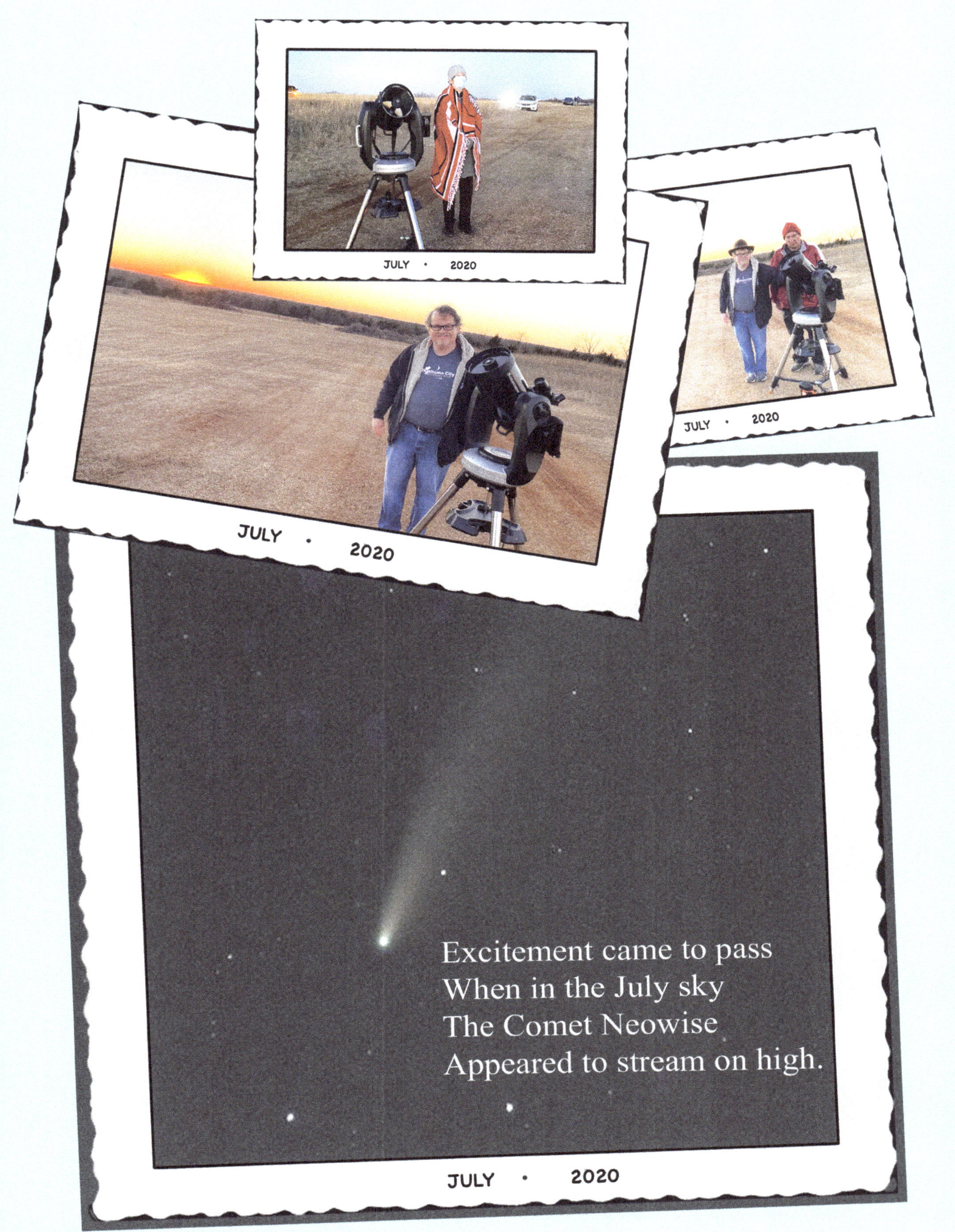

JULY • 2020
JULY • 2020
JULY • 2020
Excitement came to pass
When in the July sky
The Comet Neowise
Appeared to stream on high.
JULY • 2020

Day in and then day out,
All days appeared the same.
What weekday and what date?
We could not tell nor name.

Each week had seven days
With twelve months in the year.
We safely stayed at home
To wait for all to clear.

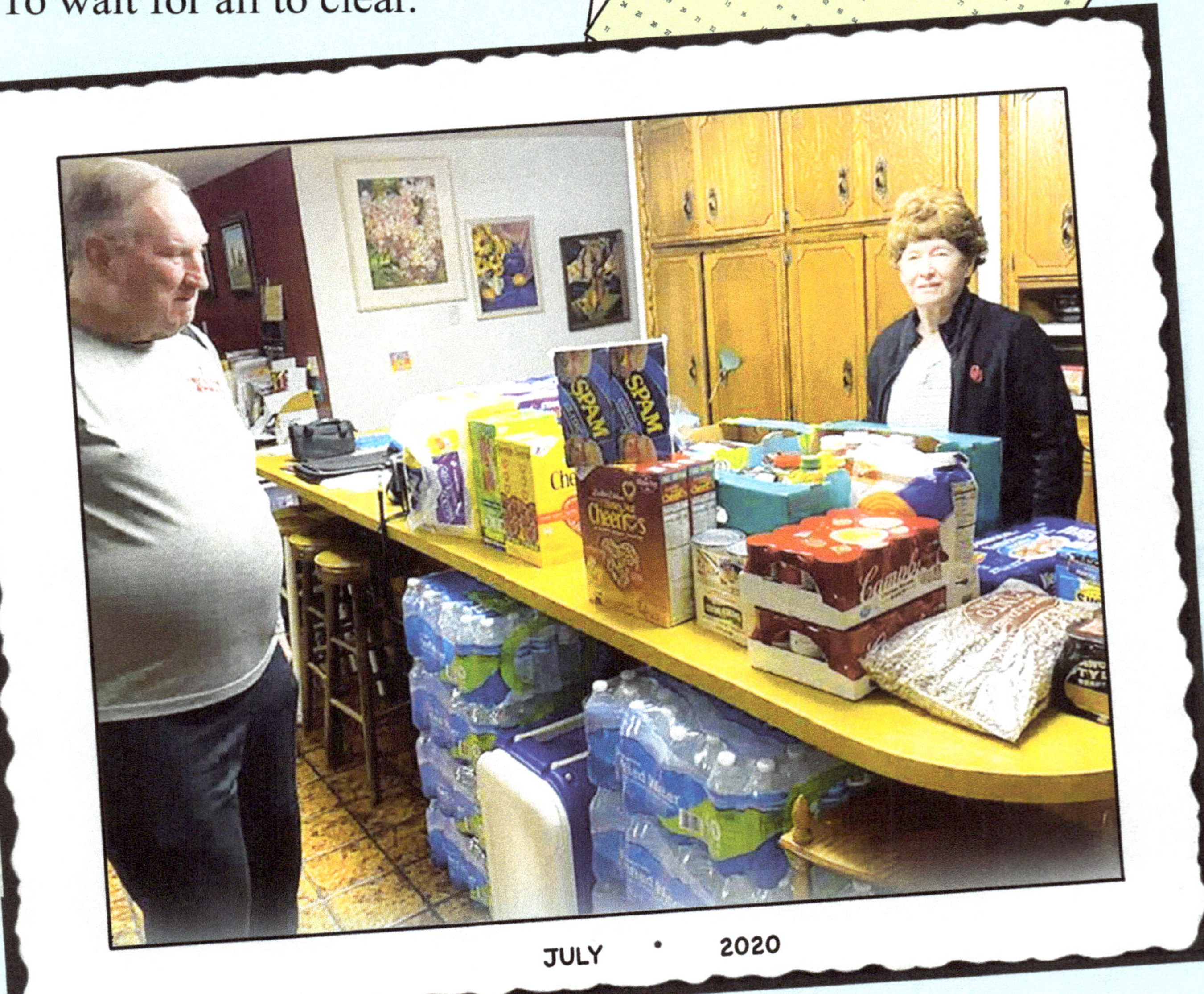

CANNED GOODS:

Beans - Baked / Black / Butterbeans
Green / Lima / Ranch / Chili
Van Camp's Pork 'n Beans / Dry

Beets
Chicken - Canned
Corn - Creamed / Whole Cut / Hominy
Fruit - Apple Sauce (no sugar added) / Apricots /
Tart Cherries / Peaches (in juice or lt. syrup)
Pears / Pineapple(Chunk - Crushed - Rings)
/ Fruit Cocktail
Mushrooms
Olives - black
Peas - Black Eyed Peas /English Peas
Peppers - Bell / Jalapeno
Pickles - Dill / Butter / Relish / Sweet / Jalepenoes
Pumpkin
Salmon - Pink Beauty (14.75 oz.)
Soup - Cream of Mushroom / Cream of Chicken
Chicken Noodle / Tomato (Campbell's)

Spam
Spinach
Stewed Tomatoes (Hunts or Del Monte)
Vienna Sausages

FRESH / FROZEN FRUITS/VEGETABLES:

Apples / Peaches / Pears / Cherries
Bananas / Strawberries / Watermelon
Frozen Blueberries / Blackberries
Oranges / Grapes / Pineapples

Broccoli / Carrots / Corn
Mixed Vegetables / Peas / Cauliflower
Onions / Okra / Beets
Peppers: Bell Peppers / Jalepeno Pepper
/ Sweet Potatoes
Potatoes
Spinach / Lettuce / Slaw
Tomatoes

PREPARED ITEMS:

Apple Cider Drink packages
BBQ Sauce
Breads - Sarah Lee 45 Calorie 100%
Whole Wheat / Hawaiian
King Rolls / Sister Schuster
Naan / Waffles / Buns
Cheese - Colby Monteray Jack /
Baby Swiss / Velveta
Chips - Tortillas / Fritos / Potato
Coffee - Decafe / Nestle's French
Vanilla Sugar-Free Coffee Mate
Cookies - Vanilla Wafer
Craisons
Crackers - Club / Graham / Ritz
Keebler Orininal Zesta Saltine
Guacamole
Ice Cream / **Sherbert**
Jello
Jelly - Blackberry
Marshmellows
Mayonaise /
Mustard   **Salad Dressing** v
Noodles - Whole Wheat Spaghetti /   (PoppySeed/Avacado)
Elbow Macaroni
Pizza
Ragu - Chunky Spaghetti Sauce
Salsa
Sour Cream / Dip
Syrup - Griffin / Blueberry / White Karo
Tea - Earl Grey / Green
Water - Bottled
Yogurt

MEATS:

Bacon
BBQ Pulled Chicken / BBQ Pulled Pork
Chicken Thighs (Skinless, Boneless)
Ground Beef (90%)
Ham
Lunch Meats: ham / turkey
Pork Chops
Sausage
Turkey / Canned turkey
Weiners -Ball Park All Beef Franks
Vienna Sausages / Bologna
1/3 lb 85% GroundSirloinBeefPatties (18)

BAKING ITEMS:

Baking Powder (60 oz.)
Baking Soda
Butter (Unsalted)
Chocolate Chips (Hershey's/Nestle
Cocoa (Hershey's)
Corn Starch (35 oz.-Argo)
Cornmeal (Shawnee's)
Craisons
Crisco (6 lbs.)
Eggs
Flour - All Purpose (12 lbs)
100% Whole Wheat
Honey - Raw
Milk - Fat Free/Skim / Powdered /
Carnation Malted Powder /
Cool Whip / Redi Whip /
Coconut milk
Nuts - Pecans-Walnuts-Almonds-
Peanuts
Oatmeal - Old Fashion Quaker Oats
Oil - Olive (Bertolli Extra Light
Tasting(2 L) / Wesson Oil
Peanut Butter - Creamy / Crunchy
Pudding - Jello / Gelatin / Tapioca
Rice - / Brown / White
Sugar - C & H granulated / Powdered /
/ Brown
Vanilla Extract
Vinegar - Heinz Apple Cider / White
Yeast

COOKING SUPPLIES:

Aluminum Foil (12x250 ft.)
Bags - Sandwich / Quart
Food Service Film (12x3000 ft.)
Melitta **Coffee Filters** (size 4)
Parchment Paper
Wax Paper

CEREALS:

Cheerios / Crunchy Pecan
Fiber One
Malt o'Meal
Raisin Bran / Rice Crispies
Nature Valley Roasted Nut Crunch-
Almond Crunch Bar
Post Toasties

___ ITEMS:

Easy 6.5 / **5.0**
Intensive Care
Old Spice / Secret (no scent)
___ons / **Cleaner**
St. Ives Renewing Collagen &
Body Lotion / Suave Vitamin
___alization Lotion / Lubridern
___mal to Dry)
Wash - Biotene / Listerine Total Care
(Purple-NOT Zero)
___rin
___rushes / **Tooth Paste** / **Floss**
___seline (7.5 oz / 13 oz)
___activ (Milk Chocolate)
Ointments - Campo-phenique / Metholatum /
Vicks Vaporub

CLEANING SUPPLIES:

All Laundry Detergent (White Container)
Cascade Dishwashing Detergent
Chlorox
Chlorox 2
Dial Complete Liquid Handsoap
Disinfectant Handywipes / Lysol Spray
Dawn Dish Liquid (Original Scent)
Germ-X Hand Sanitizing Wipes (singles)
Lysol Toilet Bowl Cleaner
Liquid Plumber
Shout
Toilet Tissue / Kleenex / Paper Towels
Trash Bags / Kitchen Tall bags

SPICES:

Lite Salt (Morton's)
Pepper
Garlic Bits / Powder
Chili Powder
Cinnamon Ground
Nutmeg
Cloves
Poultry Seasoning
Mio
Taco Seasoning
Garlic&Herb Seasoning

SWEETS:

Chocolate Chips
Hershey Nuggets
Malt Balls
M & M's Plain-Peanut
Nutter Butters
Orange Box/Mints
Oreo Cookies
Symphany Bars
Vienna Fingers
Cherry Mash

For groceries in store
We went at dawn to shop
Or internet to make
A curbside pickup stop.

Instead of eating out,
We stayed at home to eat

OATMEAL COOKIES

1. Mix until crumbly:
      1 cup shortening
      2 cups brown sugar (packed)
2. Add 2 eggs and mix well.
3. Add, then mix well:
      1 tsp. baking powder
      1 tsp. salt
      2 cups flour
4. Add 2 cups oatmeal and mix well.
      (may add 1 cup raisins)
5. Drop dough 2 inches apart and
      by a spoonful onto a greased
      cookie sheet.
6. Bake at 375°F. for 10 to 15
      minutes until browned.

BLACKBERRY COBBLER

1. Preheat oven to 350º.
2. Mix 2 cups flour and 1 1/2 tsp. salt.
3. Add 1/2 cup Wesson Oil to the flour and salt and
      mix until moistened and crumbly.
4. Add 1/4 cup milk and mix completely until it forms
      a ball.
5. Place 2 cups of blackberries in an oven-proof dish.
6. Mix together before putting over the berries:
      1/2 cup sugar
      1 Tbsp. cornstarch (or flour)
      1/2 tsp. nutmeg
      1/2 tsp. cinnamon
7. Add enough liquid (juice or water) to verily cover
      the berries.
8. While heating berries and liquid until close to boiling,
      roll out the dough.
9. First cut part of the dough to the dish size that will
      be put over the berries. Set aside.
10. Cut the rest of the dough into 1" - 2" squares.
11. Drop the dough squared into the berry-liquid mixture
      and push them under the liquid surface.
12. Place the large dough piece on top and cut slits into
      the dough, and bake until brown on top with
      juice bubbling up through the slits in the top crust.

BEST PUMPKIN BREAD EVER

1. Blend together with a mixer:
      a. 2/3 cups water
      b. 3 cups sugar
      c. 1 cup cooking oil
2. Add 4 eggs (one at a time) and continue mixing
      with the mixer.
3. Add 1 1-lb. can pumpkin and mix well.
4. Sift and Add:
      a. 3 1/2 cups flour
      b. 1 tsp. each of cloves, cinnamon, and
         nutmeg (or may use 3 tsp. Pumpkin Pie
         spice).
      c. 2 tsp. baking soda
      d. 1 1/2 tsp. salt
      e. 1 cups nuts (optional)
5. Mix well before pouring into greased and floured
      pans.
6. Fill each pan 3/4 full and bake at 350º for 1 hour.
      (To cut baking time, bake at 400º for 50
      minutes for more moist bread.)
7. Bread will freeze and thaw very well.

MY SALMON PATTIES

1. Beat 1 egg slightly.
2. Empty entire contents of 1 large can of salmon
      in bowl with egg and mix.
3. Crush 1/2 cop corn flakes and mix into the
      salmon and egg.
4. Add 1/4 tsp. pepper and mix well.
5. Form into balls and roll in crushed corn flakes.
6. Flatten each ball into a patty.
7. Add oil/Crisco to a heavy skillet and cook until
      browned.

MY MEAT BALLS

1. Beat 1 egg slightly.
2. Add 1/2 medium onion, finely diced and salt
      and pepper to taste.
3. Add and mix: 1 tsp. garlic and 1 tsp. chives,
      and 1 can stewed tomatoes, diced.
4. Mix in 1 lb. ground beef.
5. Add 1 cup oats to the mixture and mix well.
6. Roll into 1-to 2-inch balls.
7. Place in a baking dish.
8. Bake in a 400° oven for 30 minutes or until done.

MARG'S CHICKEN SALAD

1. Prepare and combine the following ingredients:
   a. Separate the chunks in 1 13-oz. can of canned chicken.
   b. Finely chop 1/3 cup onions (may use green onions).
   c. Add 1/2 cup dried canberries.
   d. Chop 1/2 cup nuts (walnuts, almond, or pecans).
   e. Chop 1 apple into small pieces (may use other fruit).
2. Add 1/2 cup of Mayonnaise (more it needed).
3. Chill in the refrigerator for an hour before serving.
4. Serve on bread of choice.

ORENE'S DEVILED EGGS

1. Boil 9 eggs, cool, shell them, and cut each lengthwise.
2. Carefully remove the yolks and mash them.
3. Add and mix well the following:
   a. 2 – 3 Tbsp. mayonnaise
   b. 1/3 onion, finely chopped
   c. 3 tsp. sweet pickle relish
   d. 2 Tbsp. catsup
   e. 1/2 – 1 tsp. salt
   f. sprinkle with black pepper to taste
4. Place 1 Tbsp. of the egg yolk mixture into each egg white.

MUSTARD POTATO SALAD

1. Boil 2 eggs, peal, and mash.
2. Cook 3 medium-sized potatoes in water, drain water, and mash.
3. Finely chop 1/2 medium-sized onion.
4. Mix eggs, onion, and potatoes.
5. Add to above mixture and mix well:
   3 Tbsp sweet pickle relish
   2 Tbsp. vinegar
   1/4 to 1/3 cup mayonnaise
   1/4 to 1/3 cup yellow prepared mustard
6. Add seasoning to the potato mixture:
   1 1/2 tsp. salt
   1 tsp pepper
   (or season to taste)
7. Cool before serving.

RICE JELLO

1. Cook rice in water but do not drain the water when cooking is completed.
   a. 1 1/2 cups long grained rice
   b. 6 cups water
2. Add, dissolve, and mix the following:
   a. 3 small packages of Jello or 1 large package of Jello
   b. 1 can (16-ounces approximately) crushed pineapple
3. Allow to set in the refrigerator until cold.
4. Stir in 12 ounces of Whipped cream.
5. Place back in the refrigerator and allow to set.

MOM'S FRIED PIES

1. Drain juice from canned fruit and add water to equal 2/3 cup if needed.
2. Mix is a separate bowl:
   1/2 cup sugar (more if desired less tart)
   2 Tbsp. cornstarch (may substitute flour)
   2 Tbsp. cinnamon
   1/2 tsp. nutmeg
   1/2 tsp. salt
3. Add enough juice to mix and dissolve sugar and the cornstarch.
4. Cook until mixture thickens. Stir frequently.
5. Cool in the refrigerator.
6. Mix together:
   2 1/2 cups flour (maybe a little more)
   1/4 cup sugar
   1 1/2 tsp. salt
   2 tsp. baking powder
7. Add 1/2 cup oil and mix until crumbly.
8. Add 1/2 cup milk and mix.
9. Knead dough slightly and roll into 2-inch balls.
10. Roll each ball into a circle.
11. Add 2 Tbsp. fruit mixture before folding over and sealing the edges.
12. Heat oil in stove-top skillet before frying the pies. After first side is browned, turn the pie over and repeat browning the other side.

And cooked old recipes
Quite easy to complete.

We worked at making pizza
And other new foods too.
Some turned out good enough
To try again to do.

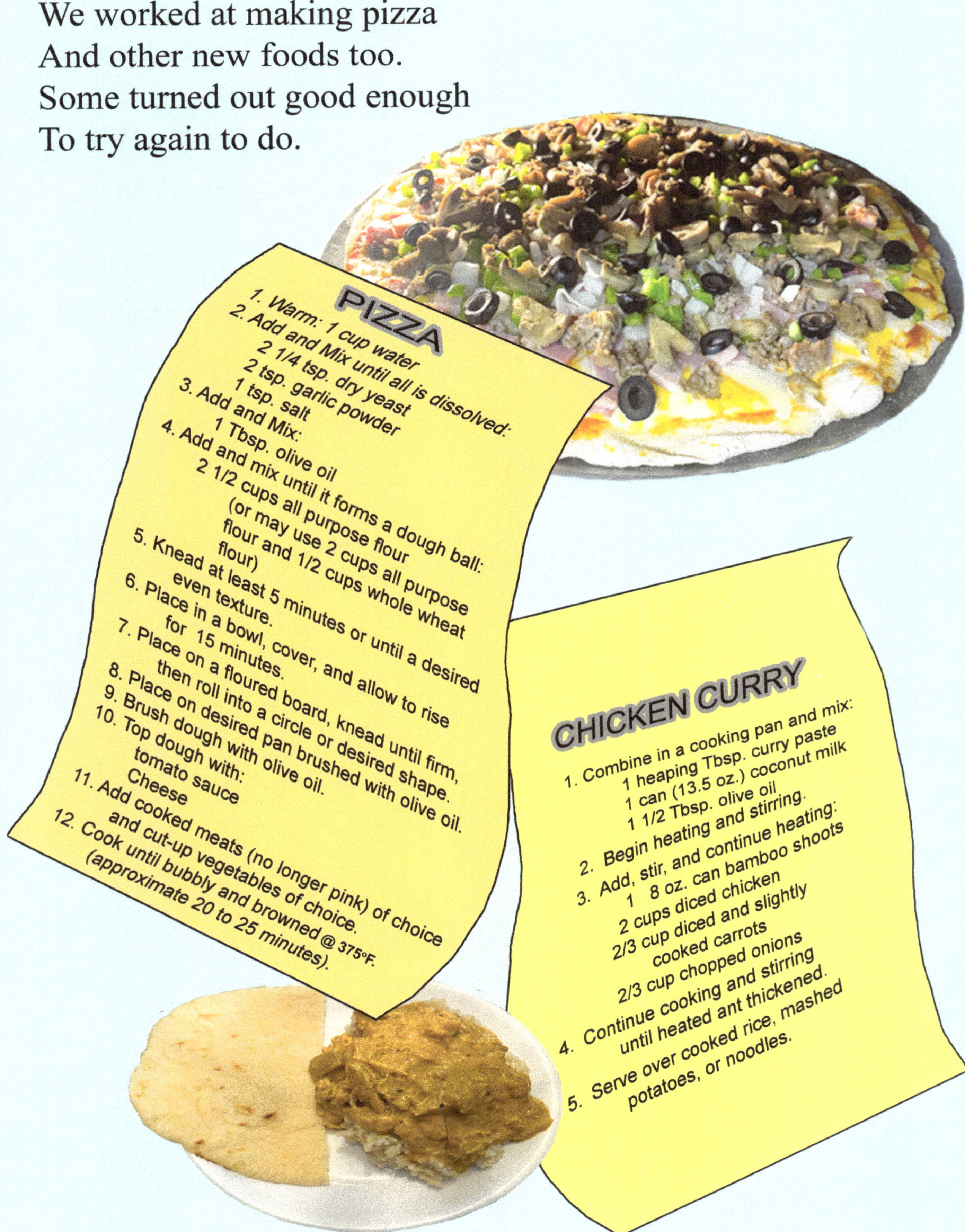

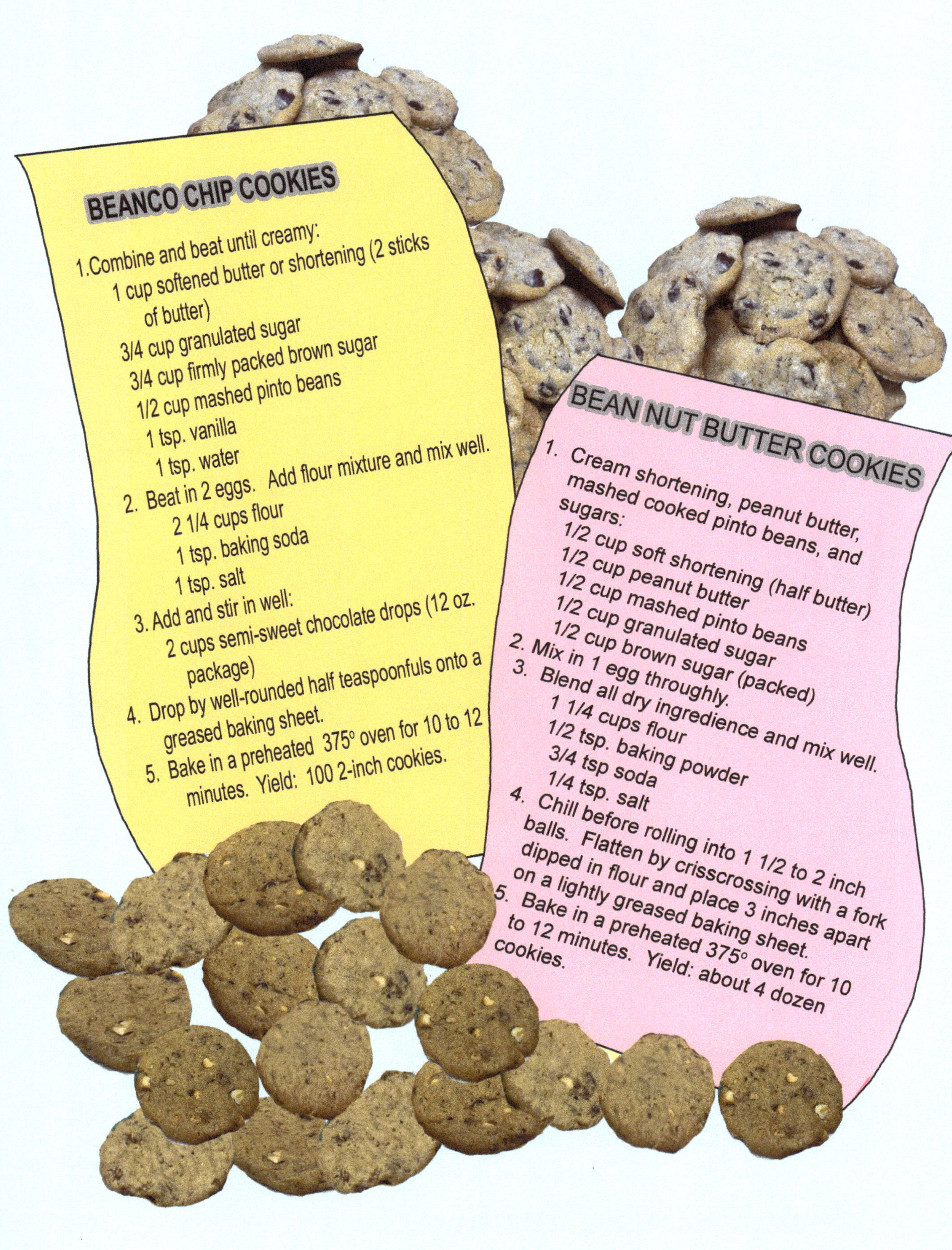

BEANCO CHIP COOKIES

1. Combine and beat until creamy:
    1 cup softened butter or shortening (2 sticks
        of butter)
    3/4 cup granulated sugar
    3/4 cup firmly packed brown sugar
    1/2 cup mashed pinto beans
    1 tsp. vanilla
    1 tsp. water
2. Beat in 2 eggs. Add flour mixture and mix well.
    2 1/4 cups flour
    1 tsp. baking soda
    1 tsp. salt
3. Add and stir in well:
    2 cups semi-sweet chocolate drops (12 oz.
        package)
4. Drop by well-rounded half teaspoonfuls onto a
    greased baking sheet.
5. Bake in a preheated 375° oven for 10 to 12
    minutes. Yield: 100 2-inch cookies.

BEAN NUT BUTTER COOKIES

1. Cream shortening, peanut butter,
    mashed cooked pinto beans, and
    sugars:
    1/2 cup soft shortening (half butter)
    1/2 cup peanut butter
    1/2 cup mashed pinto beans
    1/2 cup granulated sugar
    1/2 cup brown sugar (packed)
2. Mix in 1 egg throughly.
3. Blend all dry ingredience and mix well.
    1 1/4 cups flour
    1/2 tsp. baking powder
    3/4 tsp soda
    1/4 tsp. salt
4. Chill before rolling into 1 1/2 to 2 inch
    balls. Flatten by crisscrossing with a fork
    dipped in flour and place 3 inches apart
    on a lightly greased baking sheet.
5. Bake in a preheated 375° oven for 10
    to 12 minutes. Yield: about 4 dozen
    cookies.

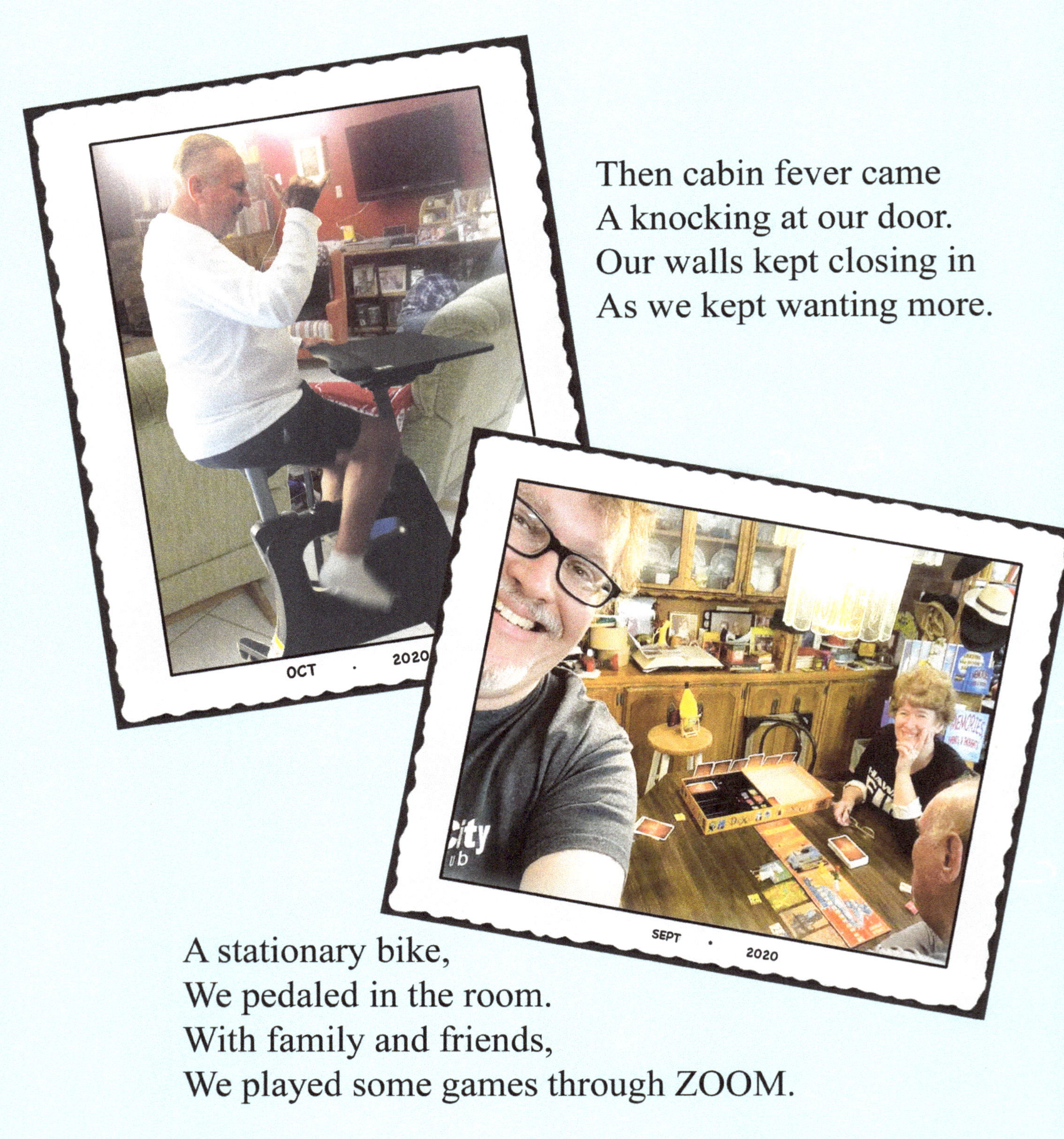

Then cabin fever came
A knocking at our door.
Our walls kept closing in
As we kept wanting more.

A stationary bike,
We pedaled in the room.
With family and friends,
We played some games through ZOOM.

At other times each day,
We cleaned or watched TV
Or phoned to talk with friends
By ZOOMING virtually.

October days of Fall,
Ablaze in red and gold,
Had shortened days of light
And weather turning cold.

It started out as rain
Which soon began to freeze
With weight that broke some limbs
On trees still bearing leaves.

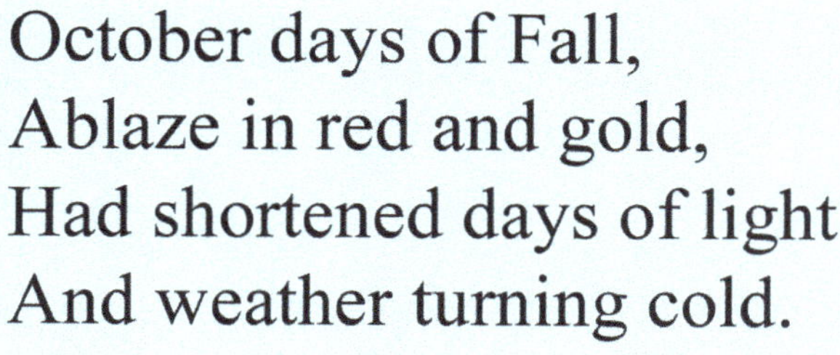

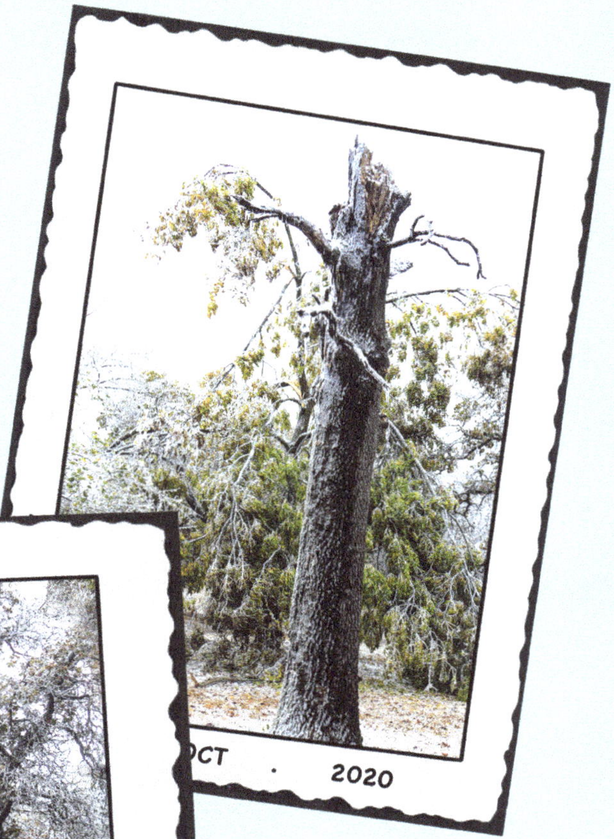

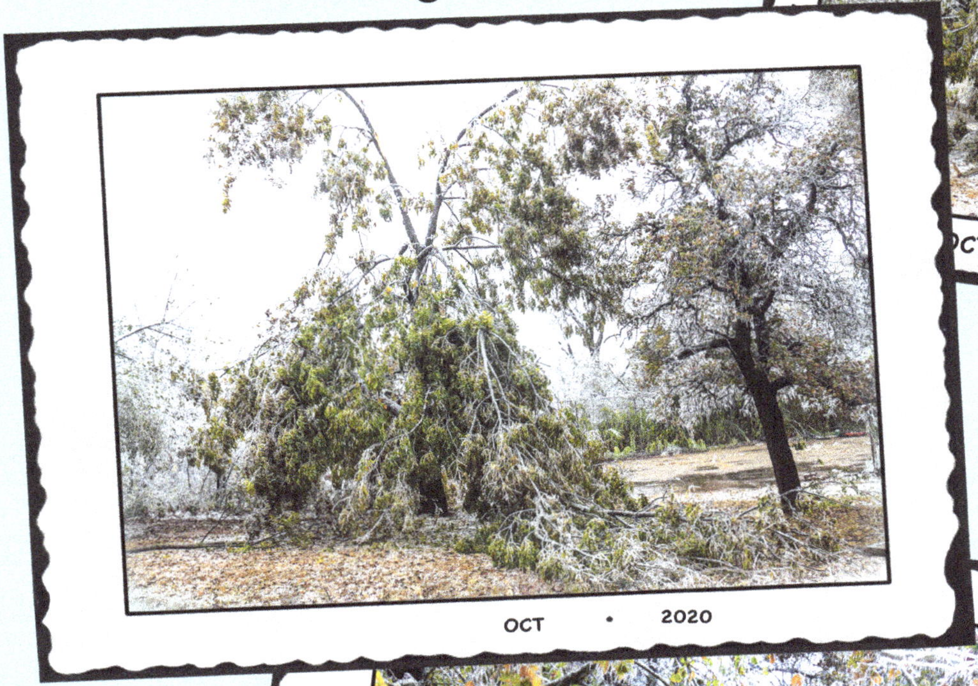

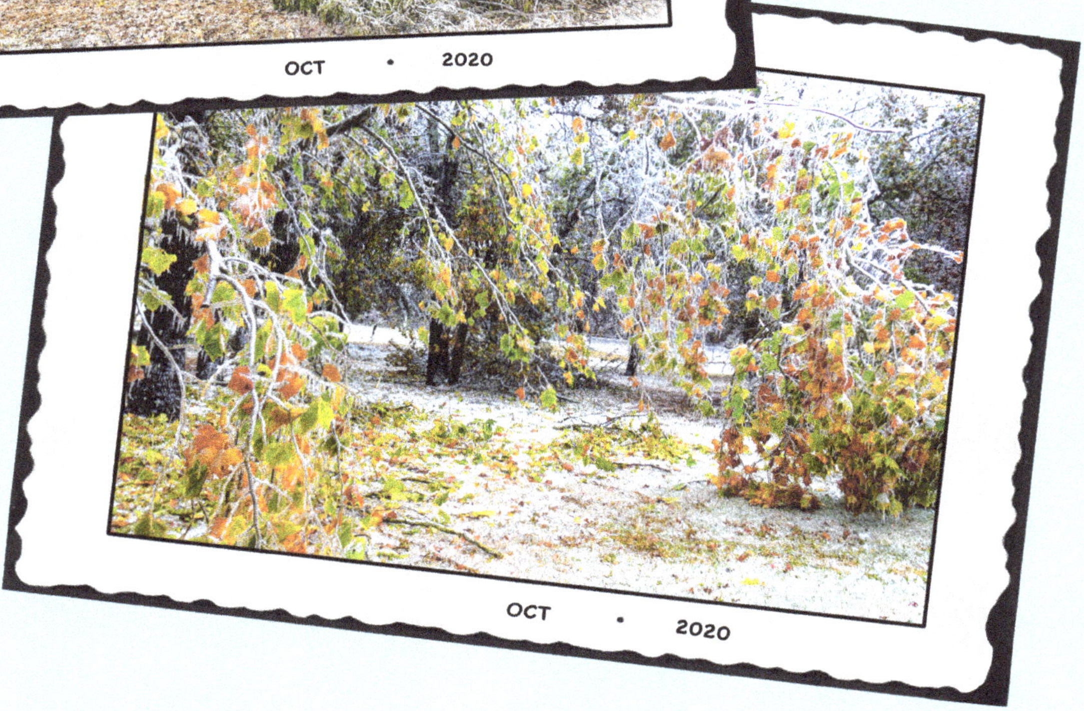

A blue moon rose on Halloween
With clearing skies just right.
We dressed in costumes fitting
To celebrate the night.

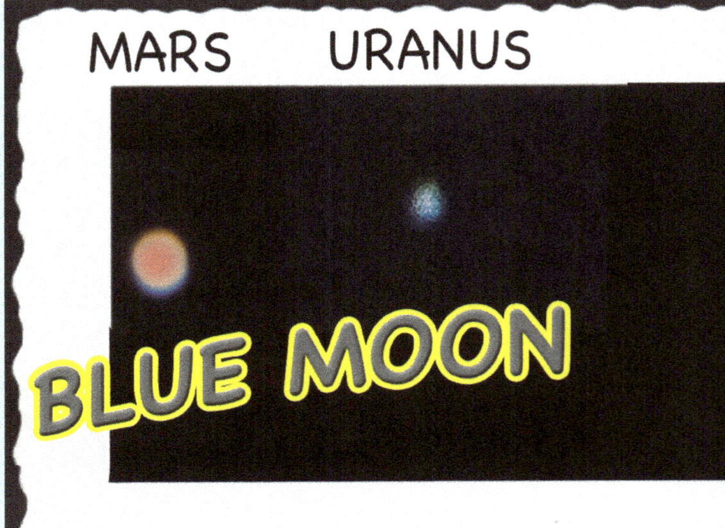

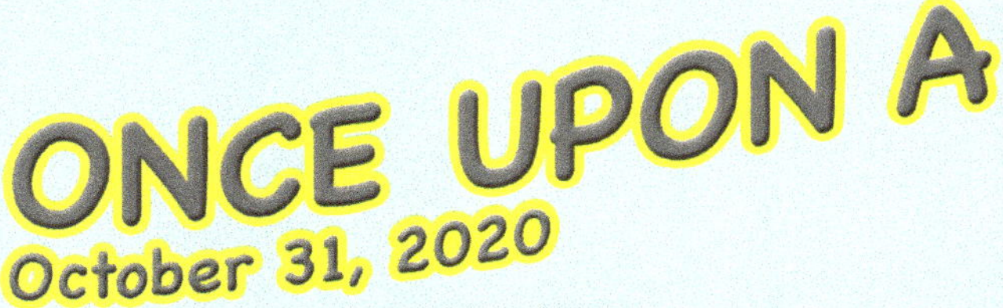

Our telescope we set
For scanning southern skies
Where we could focus in
Upon our viewing prize.

The planet Jupiter,
With swirling stripes so bright
And moons that orbit it,
Came first into our sight.

Then next we looked at Saturn,
That twinkled in the sky
Encased in golden rings,
So tiny there on high.

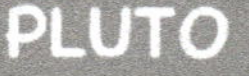

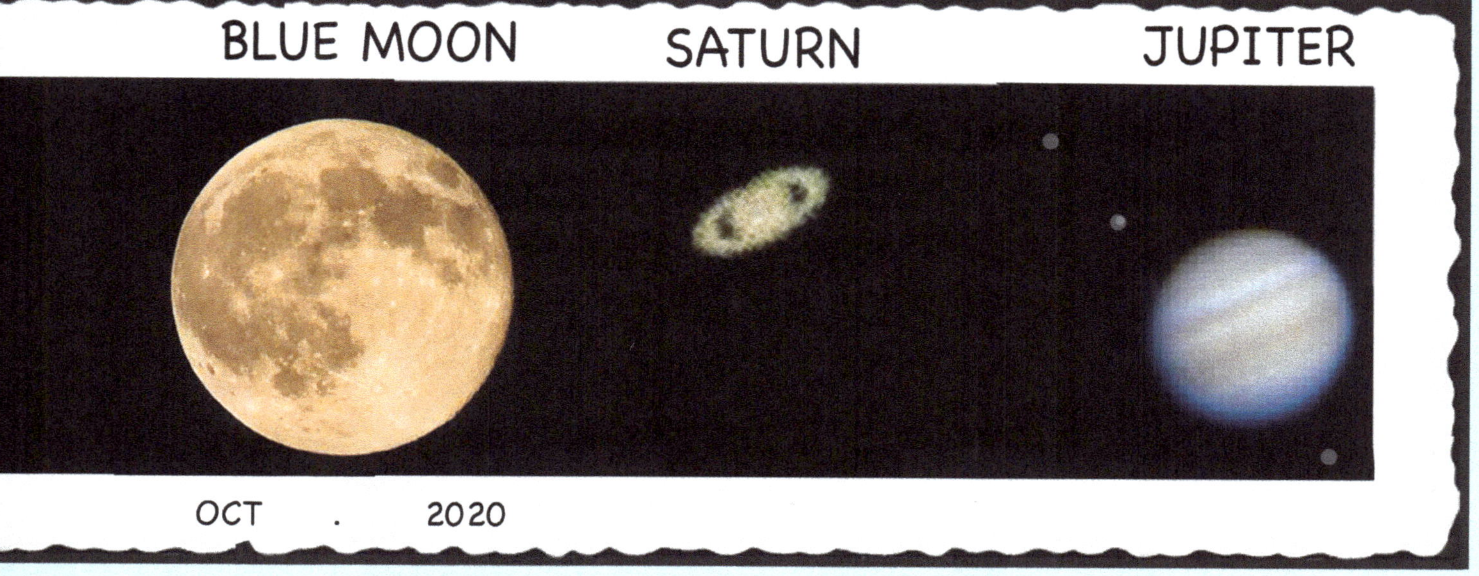

Ascending in the east
Where hanging clouds had cleared,
The reddish body form
Of planet Mars appeared.

Then next we found Uranus,
So fuzzy to the eye,
And difficult to say
We did identify.

About that time came Pluto,
Demanding his due care.
With ball in mouth, he bid
A game of fetch to share.

BACKGROUND INFORMATION:

Once upon a Blue Moon (10.31.2020), Jer set up his telescope so that
we could see the planets: Mars, Saturn, Jupiter, & Uranus. We also
saw Pluto...and I played kickball with him to keep him away from
the telescope. He is always bringing his ball over and it's so wet from
being in his mouth.
I also dressed up for Halloween in a costume I hadn't worn for ten
years. The last time we were enjoying Halloween in Waikiki and our
costumes had the crowd humming the Pink Panther theme with us!

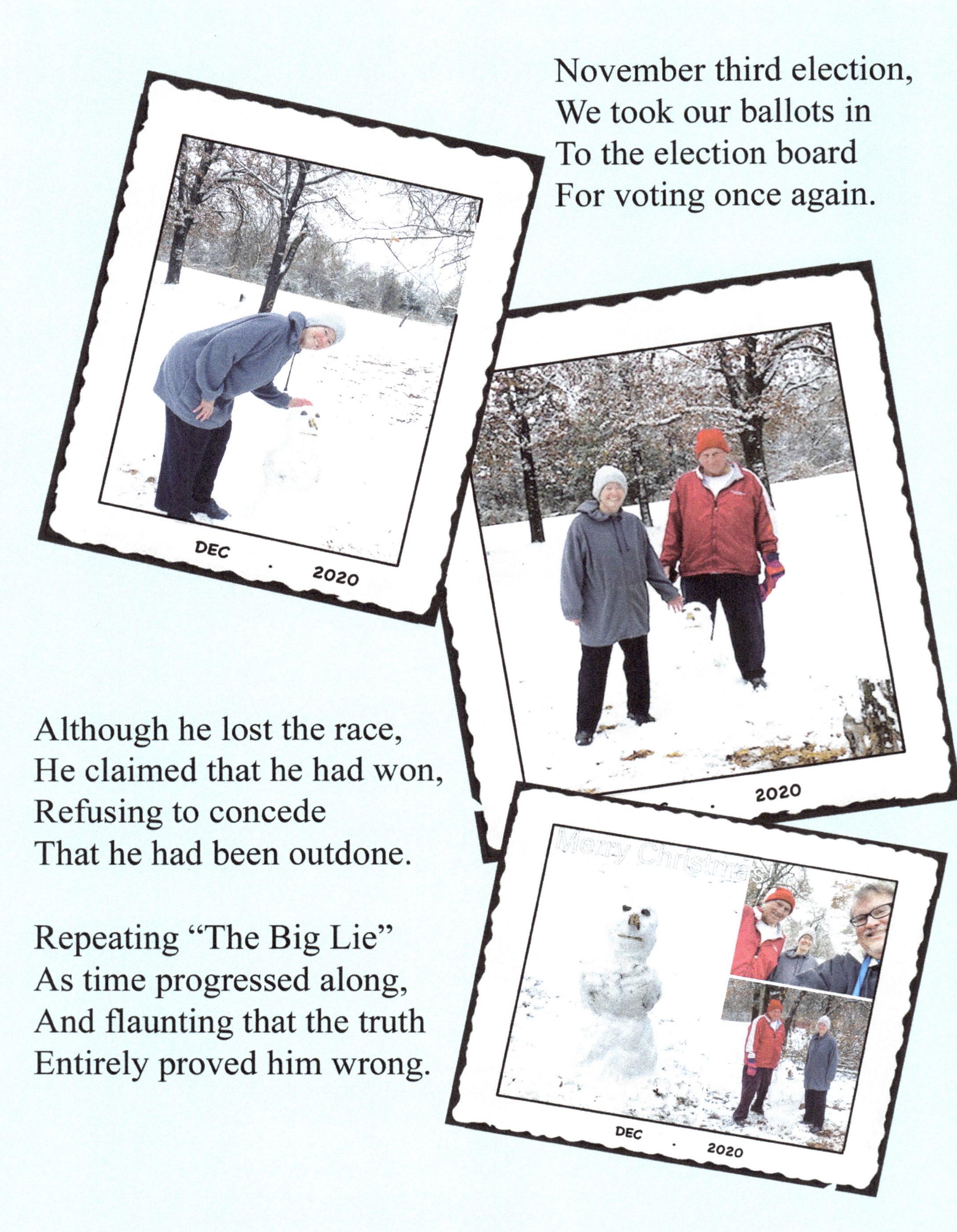

November third election,
We took our ballots in
To the election board
For voting once again.

Although he lost the race,
He claimed that he had won,
Refusing to concede
That he had been outdone.

Repeating "The Big Lie"
As time progressed along,
And flaunting that the truth
Entirely proved him wrong.

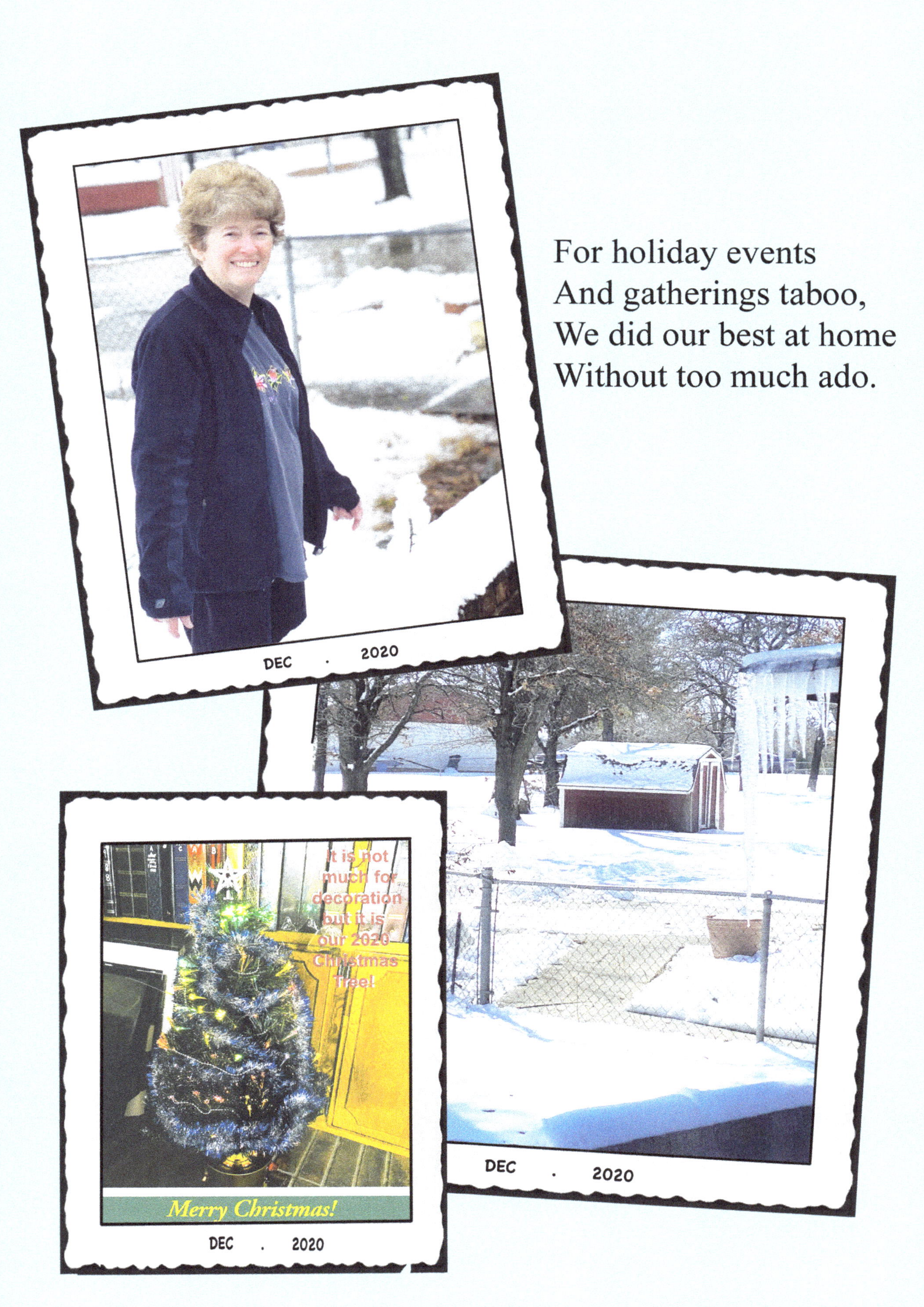

For holiday events
And gatherings taboo,
We did our best at home
Without too much ado.

December news reported
Vaccines would be dispersed,
But only certain groups
Could get their shot at first.

The year of twenty-twenty
Developed a great cost
In businesses that failed
And friends and family lost.

Goodbye to twenty-twenty
With all its deadly scope,
Shutdowns, and quarantines,
But never losing hope.

The year of twenty-twenty,
Its dark and daunting days,
Kept us from kin and friends
Transforming normal ways.

So many virus victims
Found all around the sphere,
But U.S. lack of leadership
Caused it most deadly here!

So many died from Covid
Or faced a body ill.
Some suffered not at all,
While some escaped it still.

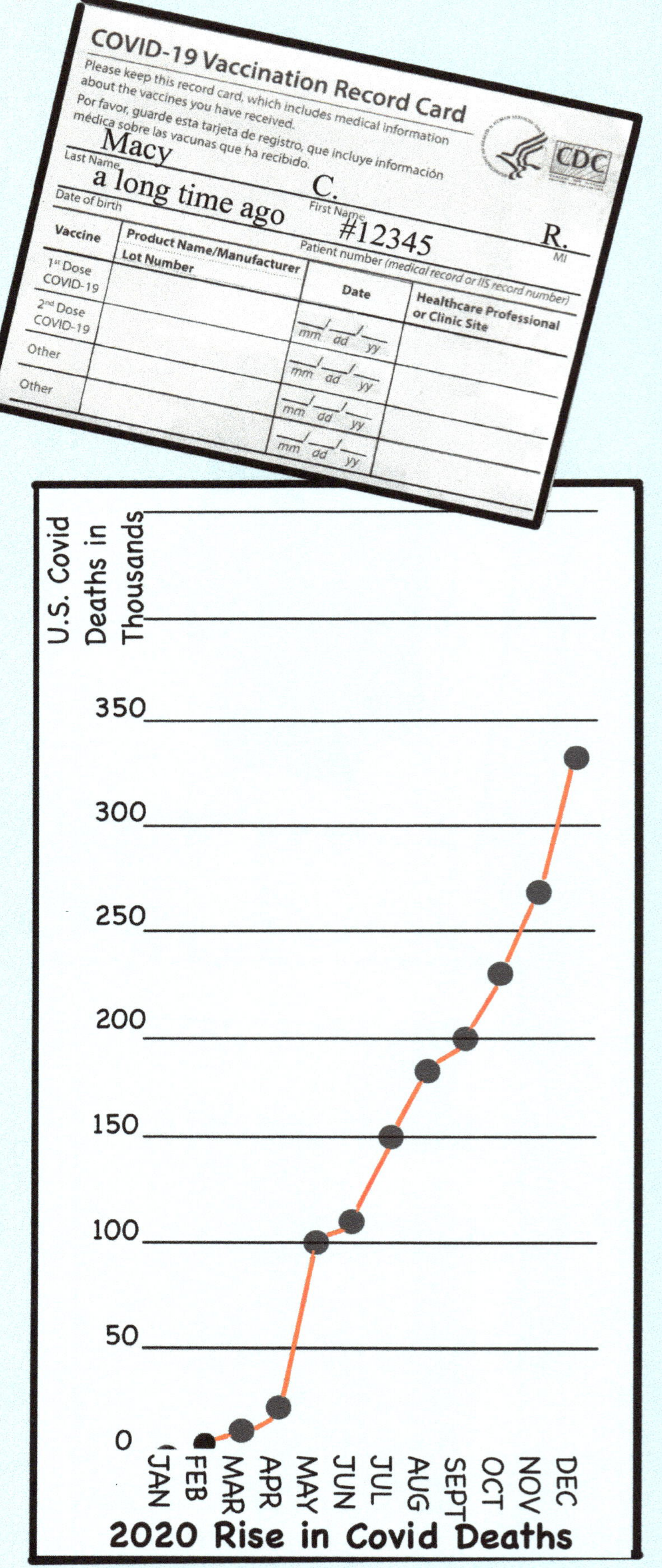

Supreme Court nominees
Picked by the President,
Awaited confirmation
By Senate vote consent.

Within his term in office,
He nominated three
Supreme Court Justices
But chose them recklessly.

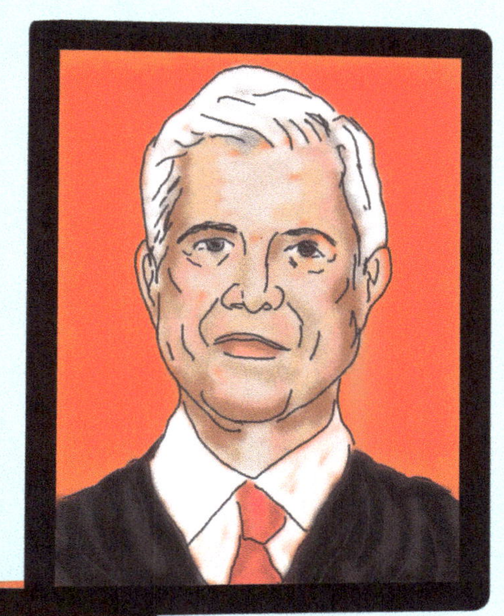

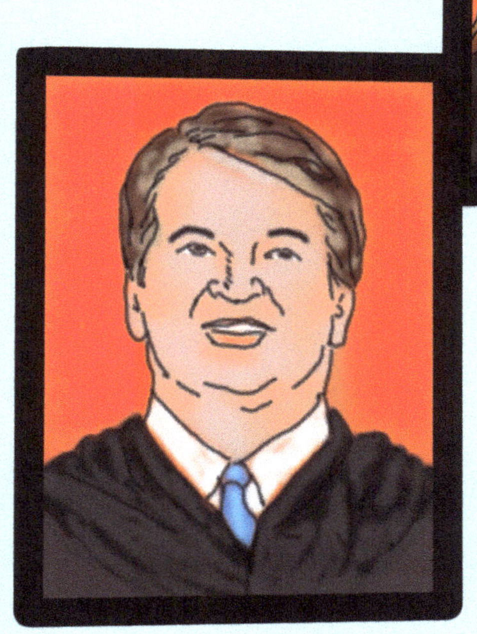

The senate quickly voted
For nominees he picked.
We later found they lied
On things they would restrict.

May last year be forgotten
As New Year brings us hope.
May troubles fade away
With blessings in our scope.

JANUARY 2021

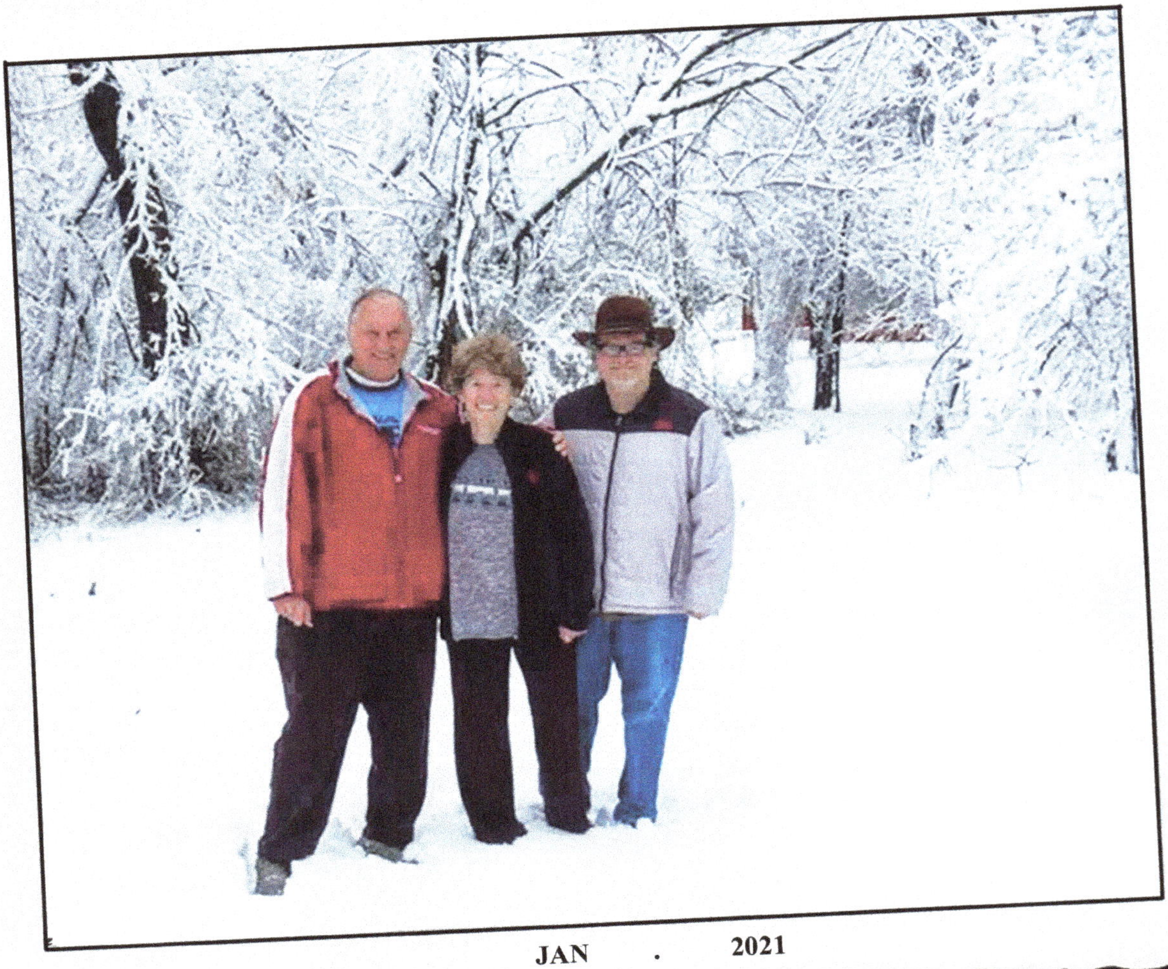

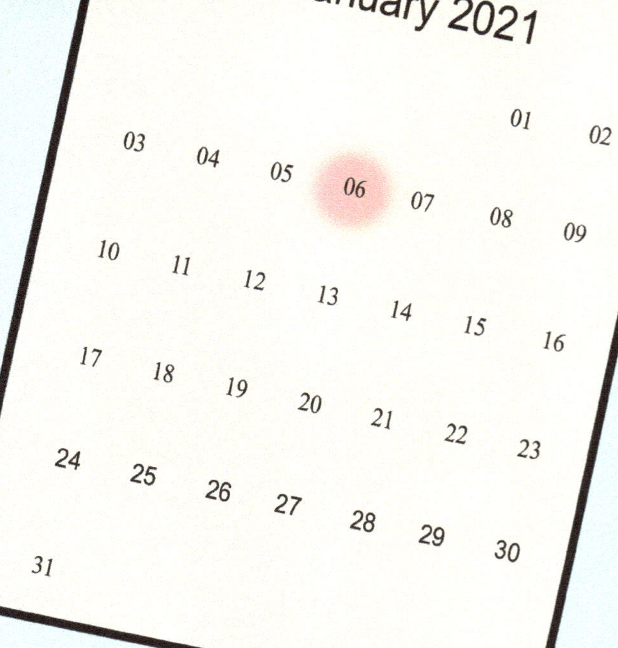

As twenty-twenty ended
And night began to fall,
A freezing rain commenced
With glazing overall.

The New Year ushered in
Completely white with snow.
It covered up the ice
The old year put below.

On January sixth
In twenty-twenty-one,
The White House held a rally
Declaring he had won.

He asked the crowd for help
To fight for what was right
For they could "Stop the Steal"
If they would all unite.

He safely fled to watch
The White House TV set
And marveled at the sight
Of actions he beget.

For many hours police,
Though battered and outdone,
Held off the frenzied crowd
To then be overrun.

They stormed the Halls of Congress.
This crowd became a mob
That vandalized and threatened
The Congress at its job.

That day the Congress met
To certify each state's
Still sealed elector ballots
For both the candidates.

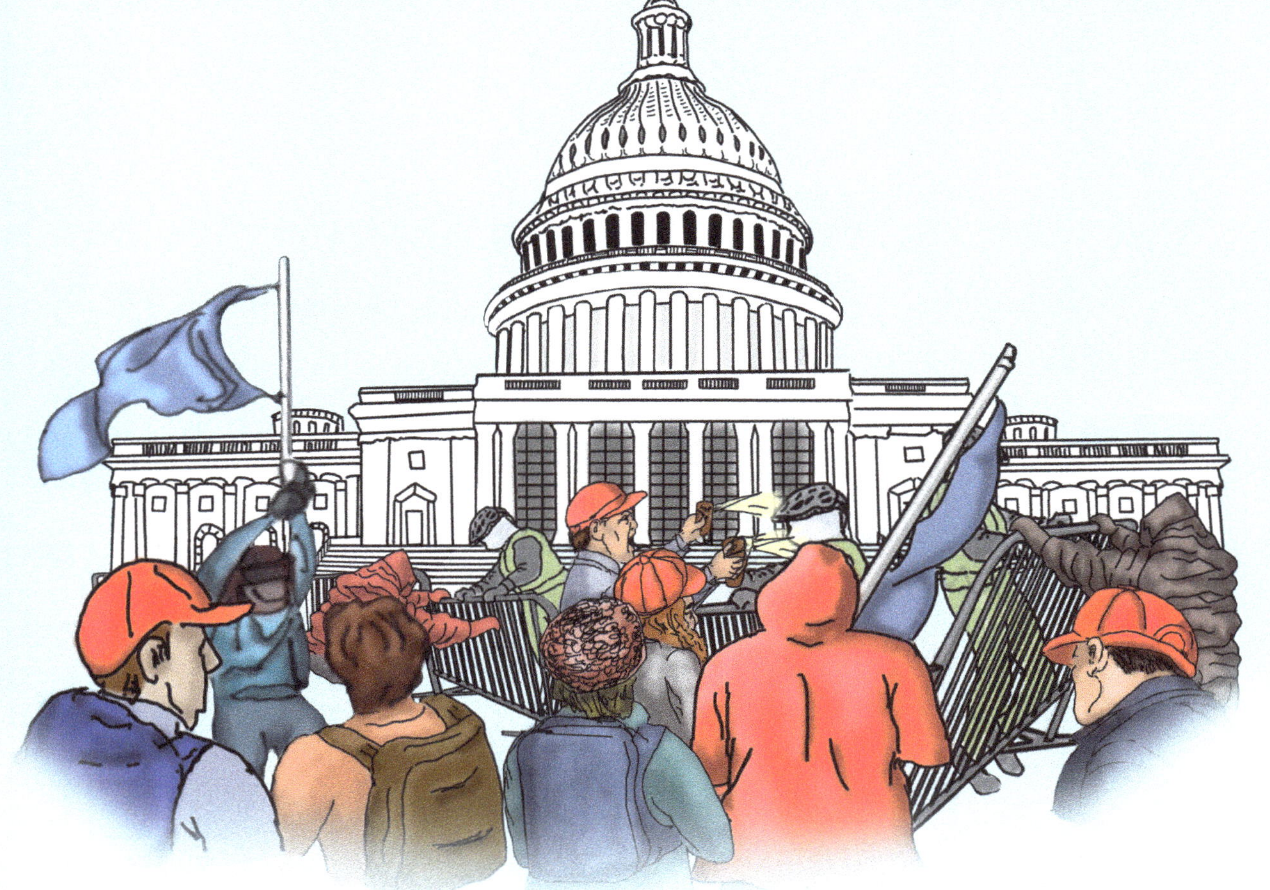

The Congress fled to safety
Until the threat was done,
Then counted all the votes
Which proved that Biden won.

Refusing to concede,
He then refused to go
To the inauguration
For peaceful change to show.

Then lawsuit after lawsuit,
The courts denied each one
As frivolous and that
No voting fraud was done.

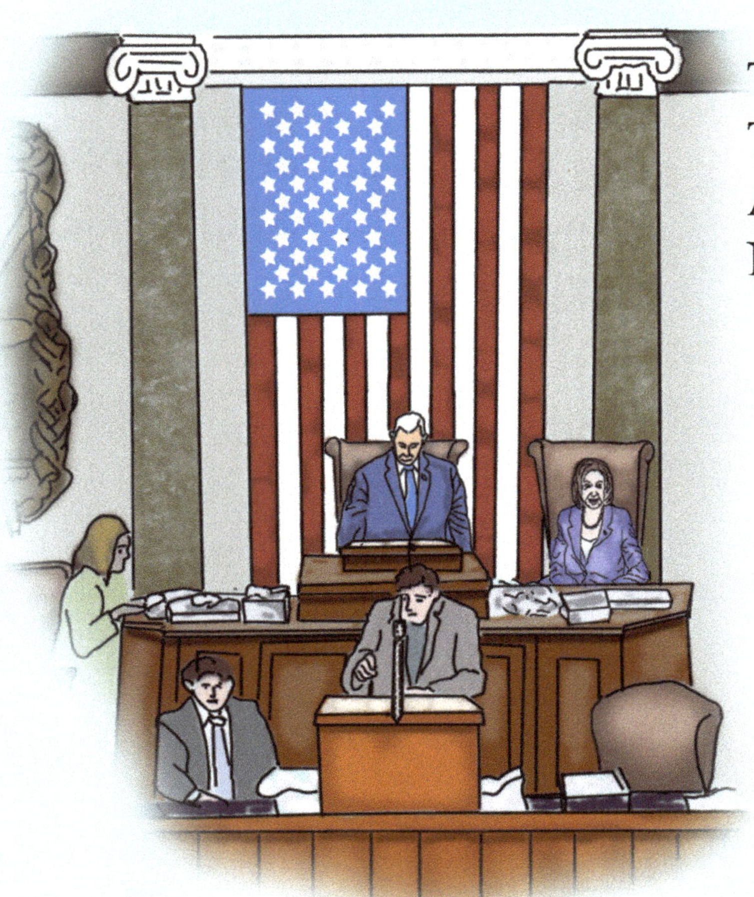

For his obstructing Congress
In duties they must do,
And his abuse of power,
Impeachment followed through.

Again, the Senate voiced
Those charges didn't fit.
Along a party line,
They voted to acquit.

For time and place, we searched
The web site for a spot
And traveled miles from home
To get our vaccine shot.

Next month again, we searched
The web site for a spot
And traveled miles from home
To get our second shot.

Some quacks put fear in folks
Through telling ugly lies
About the new vaccine.
That caused a death toll rise.

Our next door neighbor died.
Some kin came down with it,
But most had both their shots,
Which proved a benefit.

And after many months
Of letting hair grow wild,
In May we made appointments
To have it cut and styled.

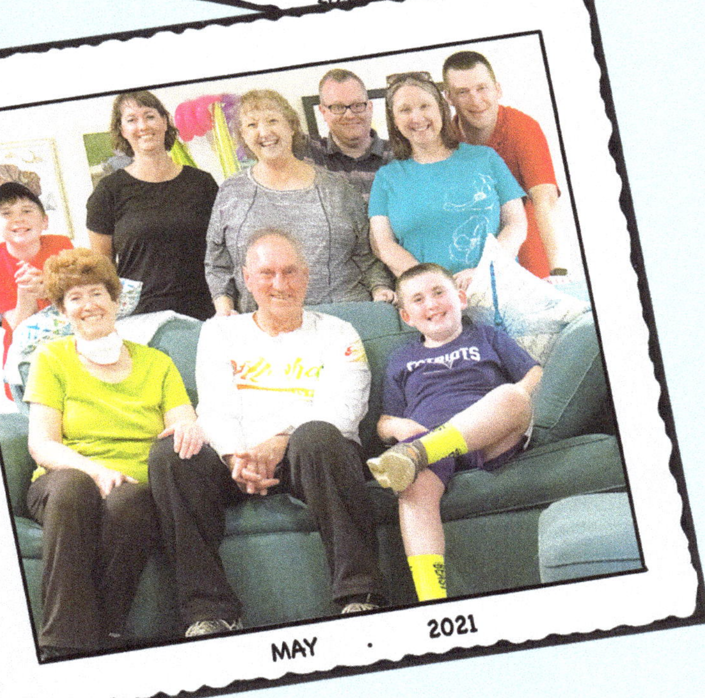

When Covid cases slowed,
We went to see some kin
And then a place or two
To see each place again.

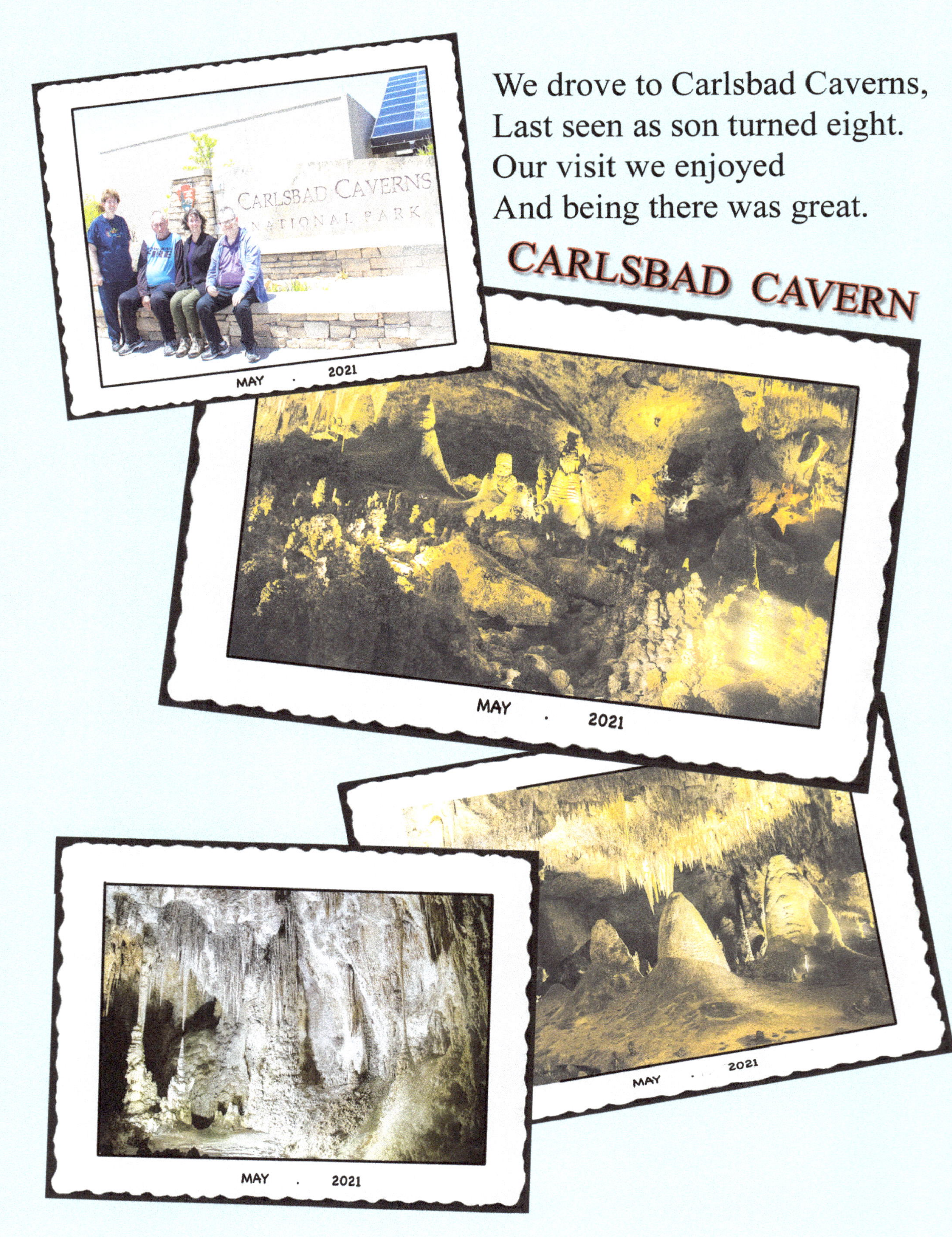

We drove to Carlsbad Caverns,
Last seen as son turned eight.
Our visit we enjoyed
And being there was great.

CARLSBAD CAVERN

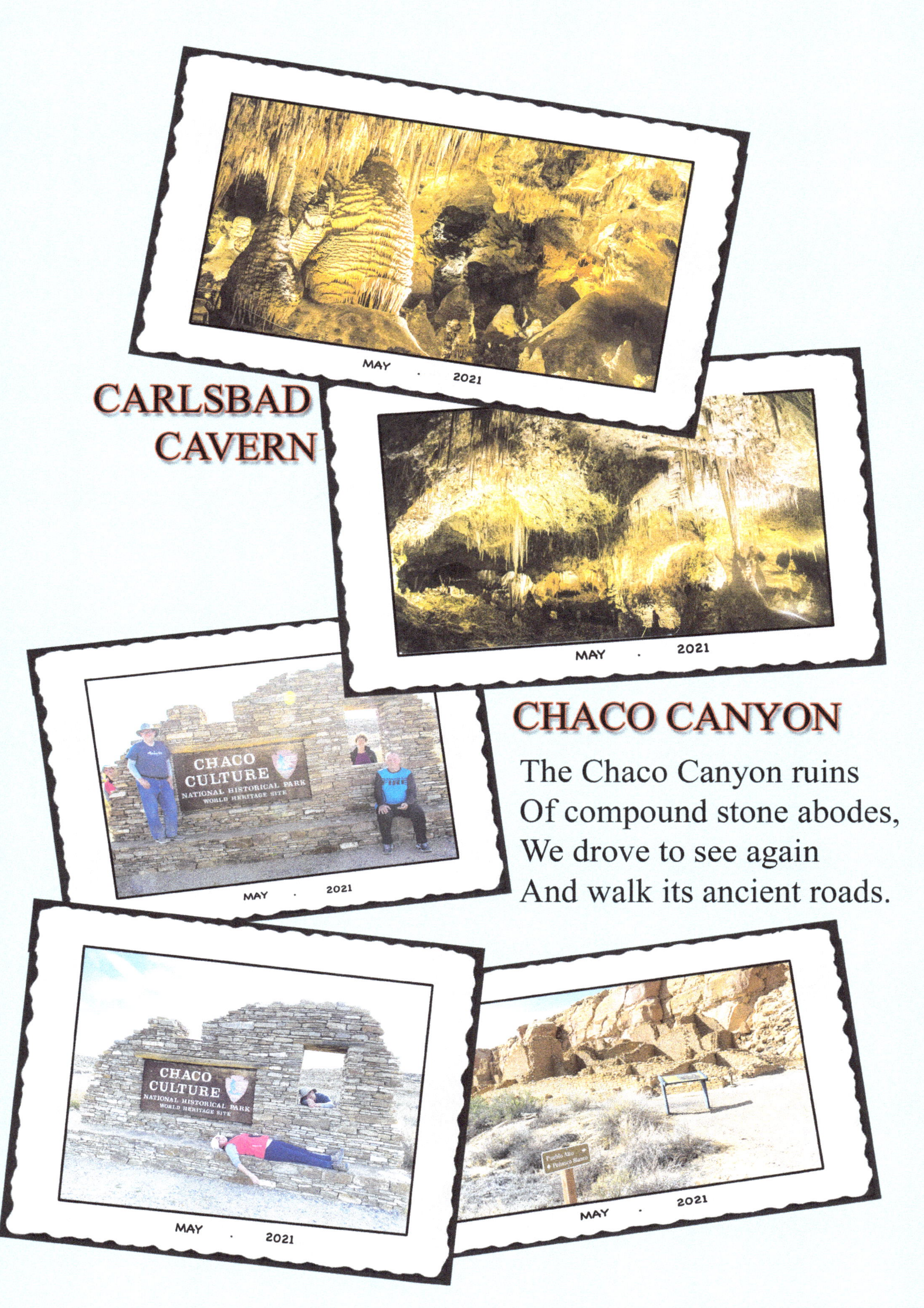

CARLSBAD CAVERN

CHACO CANYON

The Chaco Canyon ruins
Of compound stone abodes,
We drove to see again
And walk its ancient roads.

CHACO CANYON

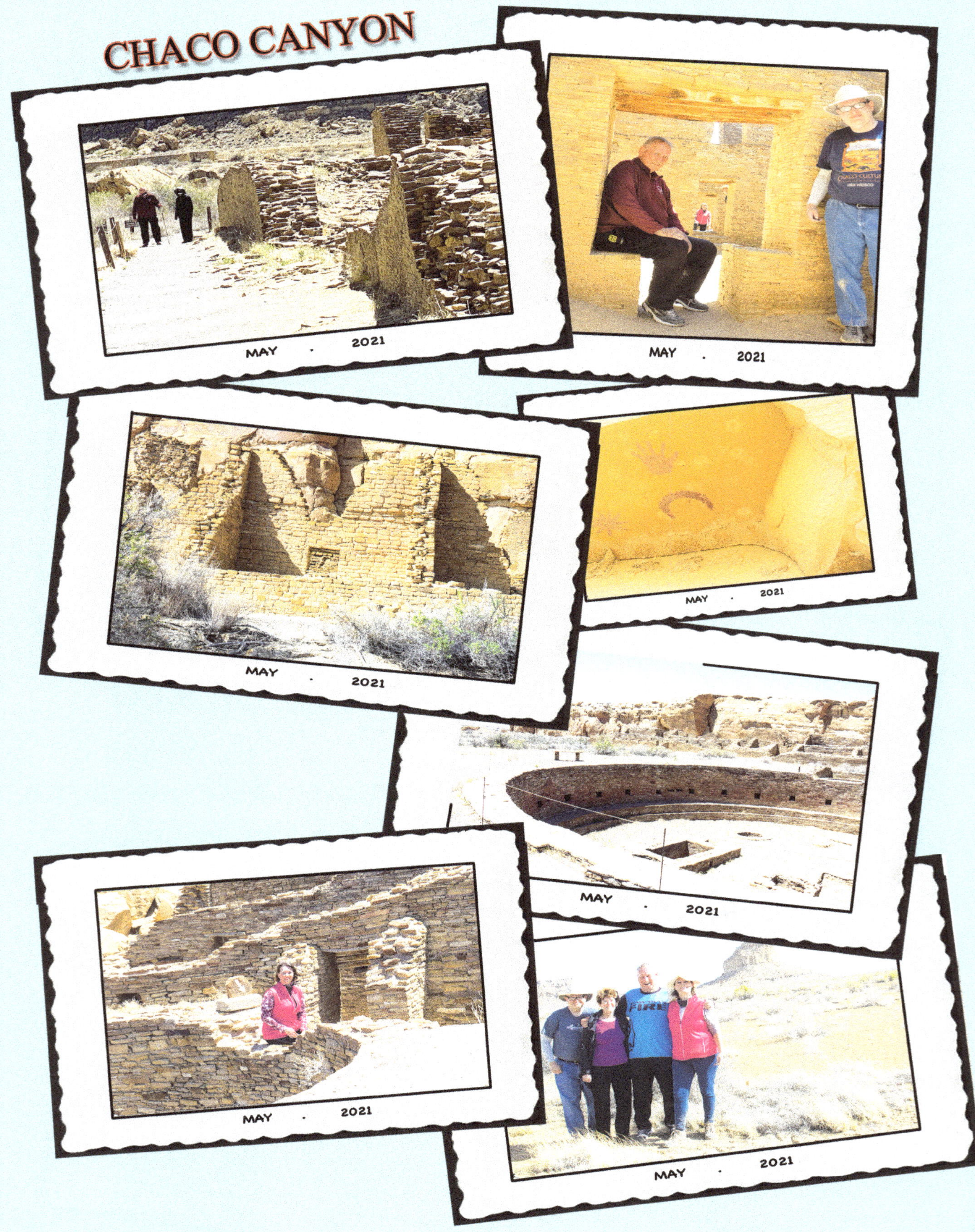

A new and mutant form
In May appeared to strike
Unvaccinated folks
Of young and old alike.

This delta mutant form
More deadly than before,
Attacked those with no shot
To raise the death toll more.

Then folks that took both shots
Began to come down ill.
With milder symptoms shown,
They swiftly mended still.

Then after July fourth,
The virus spread grew wide.
Again hospital beds
Became all occupied.

Those folks refusing shots
Became the target host.
The virus as it spread,
Affected them the most.

Still anti-vaxors screamed,
"No vaccine and no mask!"
Hospitals started struggling
And could not do their task.

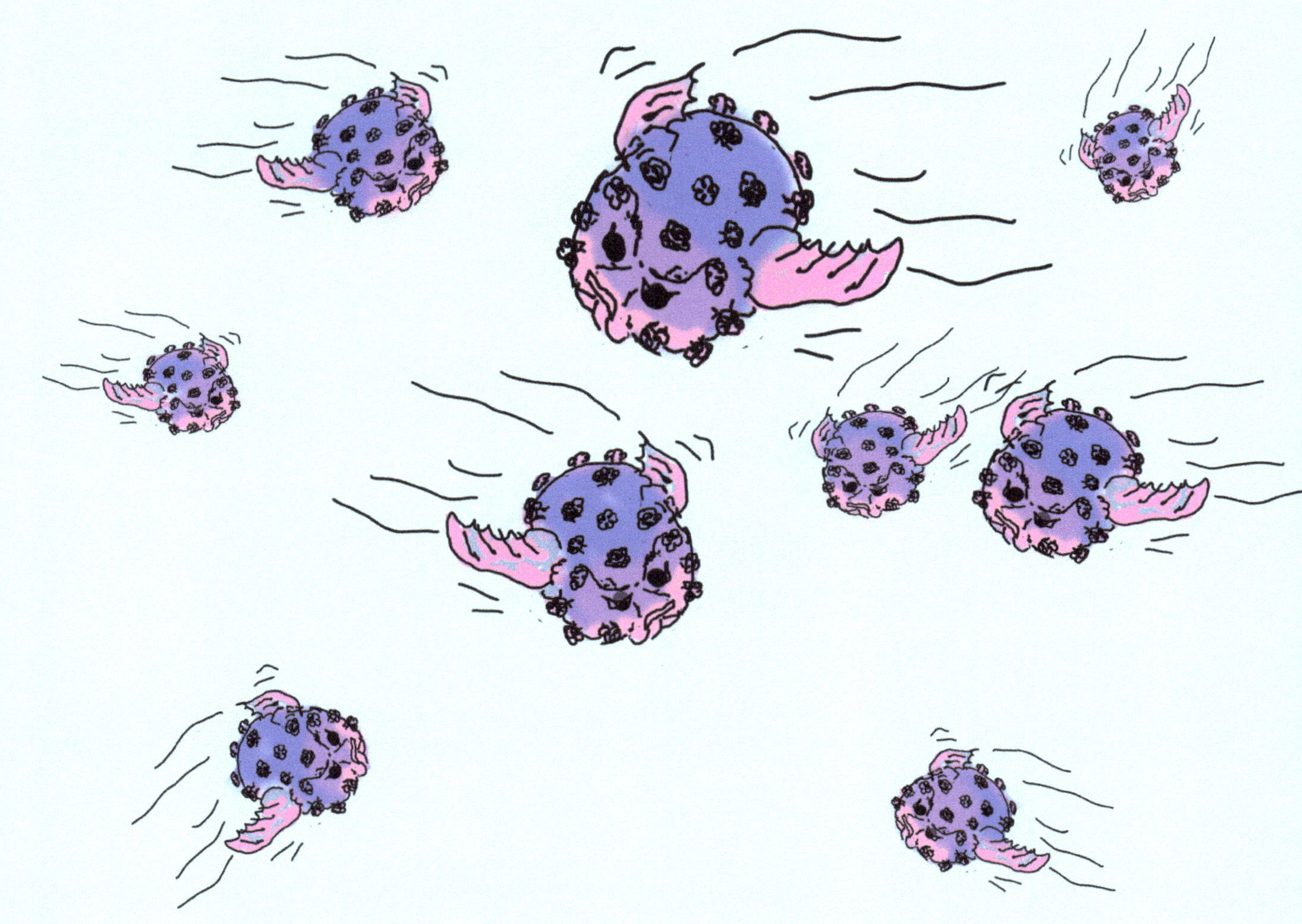

The last of August saw
Our longest war to date
Come to a final end
And troops evacuate.

Fall schools began again
With Covid on the rise.
Some parents yelled, "No mask!"
With freedom as their guise.

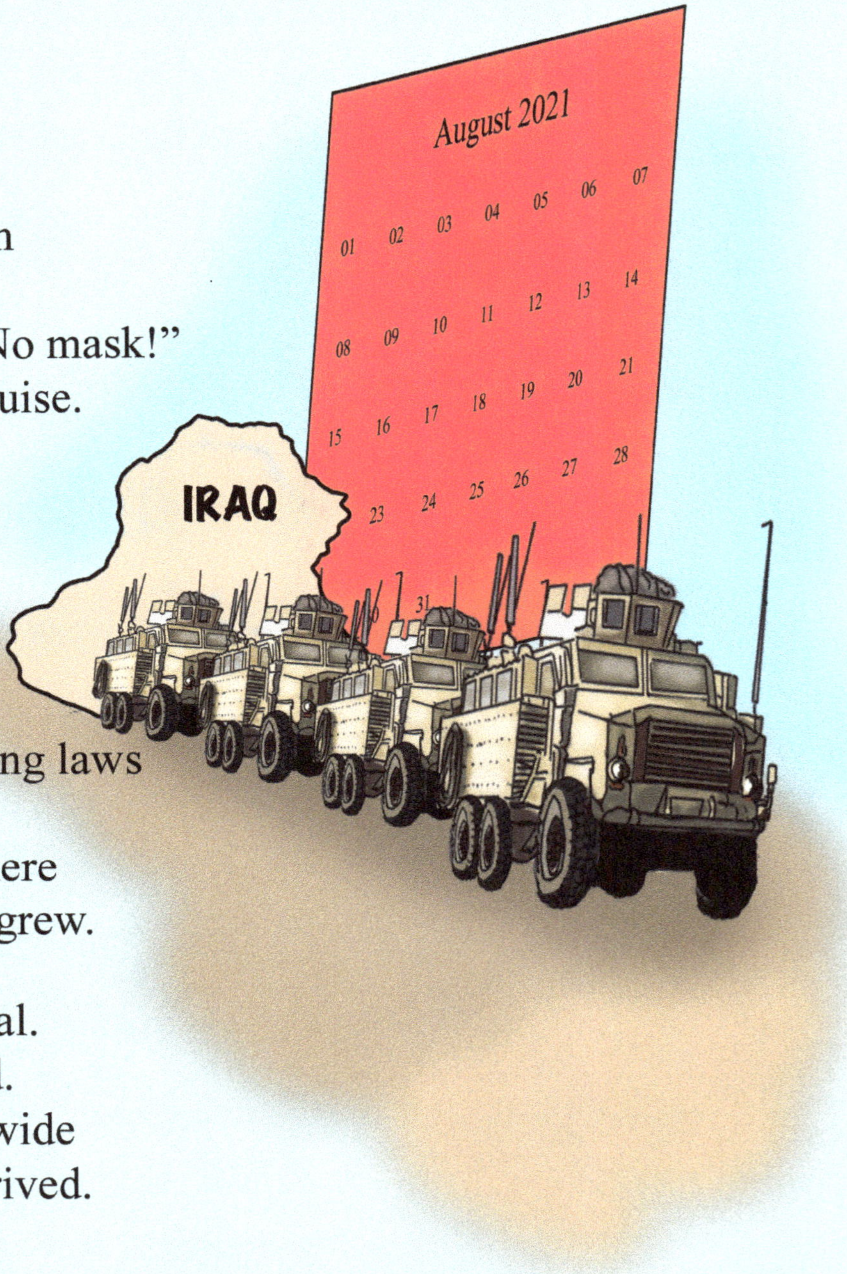

All-out assault began
On our democracy
By voting to suppress
Or topple liberty.

Some states passed voting laws
To make it hard to do
And gerrymandered where
Their winning chances grew.

Court cases came to trial.
Misinformation thrived.
The lie spread far and wide
With voting rights deprived.

Attacking schools began
About what could be taught.
Some laws were put in place
To stop what they should not.

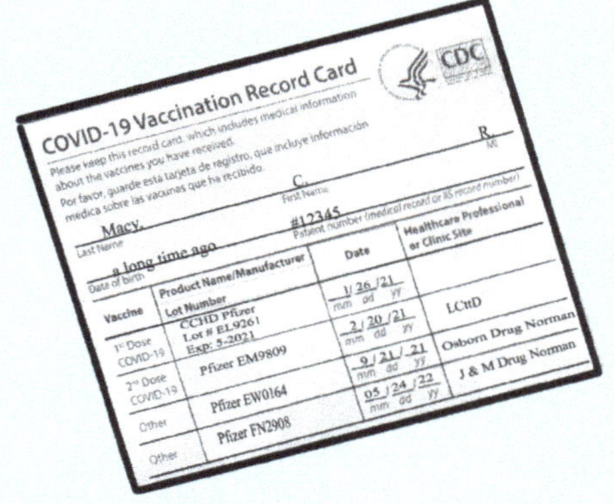

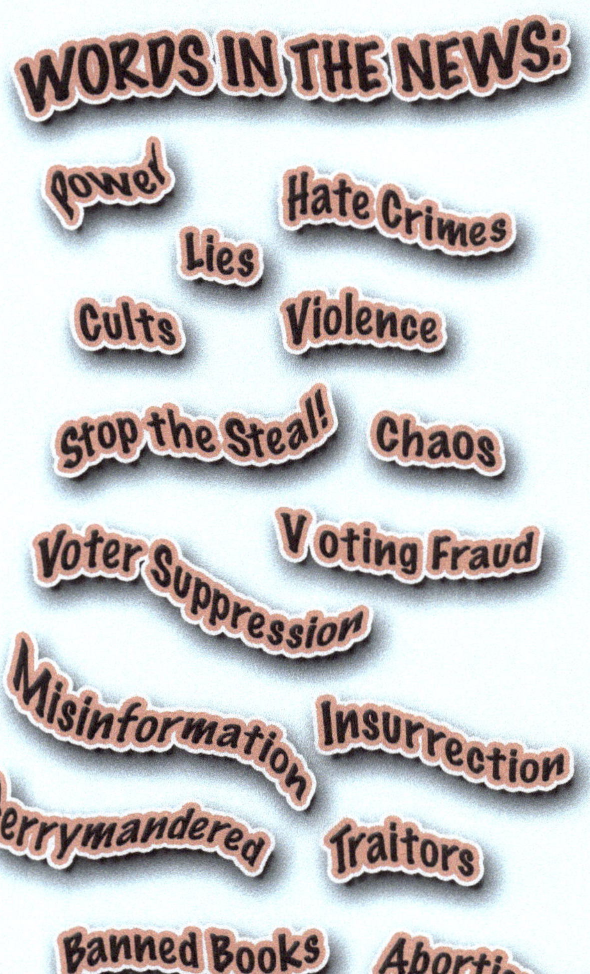

The CDC announced
Those over sixty-four
Could get a booster shot
That would protect them more.

The filibuster made
Republicans a blight
By voting "No" and choosing
For power over right.

The lying loser still
Continued on his way
With rallies, hoaxes, madness,
Forever and a day.

His followers became
A cult to do his will.
They broke the law for him
And do his bidding still.

Some groups used fear and force
To "Stop the Steal", they cried.
They blamed election folks
With voting fraud implied.

These groups then in our nation,
Provoked by deadly lies
And spurred by hate, caused threats
Of violence to rise.

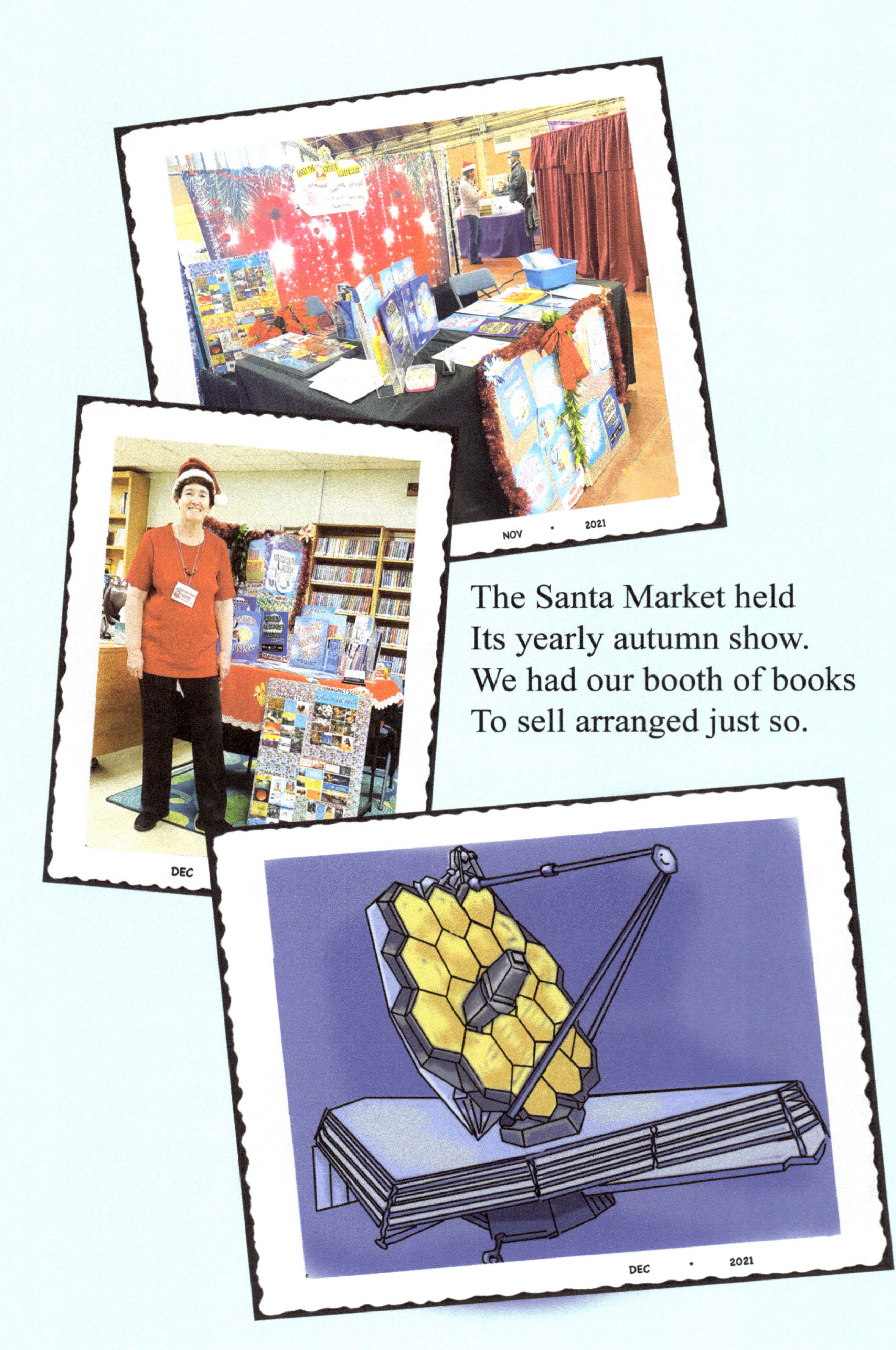

The Santa Market held
Its yearly autumn show.
We had our booth of books
To sell arranged just so.

With crowds taboo last year,
Events did not take place.
My hometown library
This year gave me a space.

The James Webb telescope,
They launched on Christmas Day.
It held the hope of gaining
New knowledge far away.

This climate changing year
Brought fierce tornado bouts,
More hurricanes and flooding,
With many fires and droughts.

The covid omicron
Appeared in twenty-one
At the year's end to make
Hospitals overrun.

Democracy at risk,
Pandemic causing fears,
And isolation felt
Sums up these last two years.

But yet we carry on
And take each day in stride.
In looking back, the time
Has quickly passed aside.

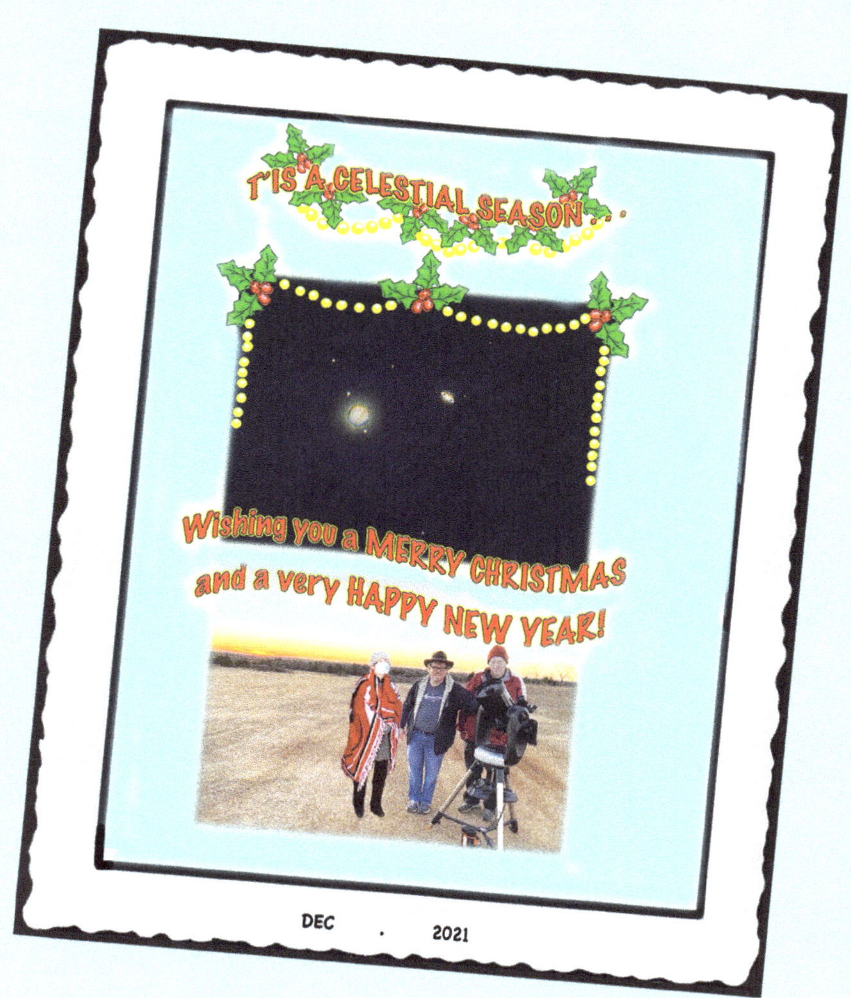

JANUARY 2022

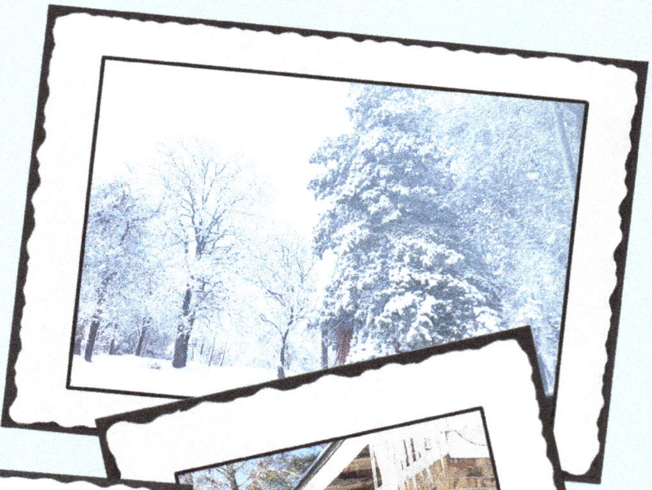

As history repeats
On New Year's Eve again,
Some moisture fell as rain
Before the snow came in.

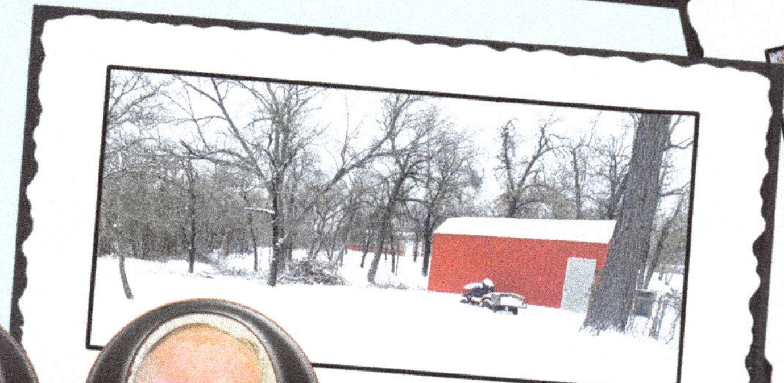

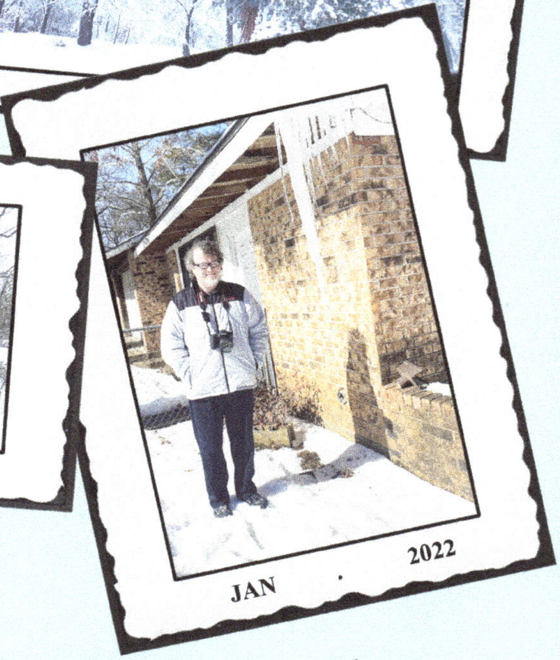

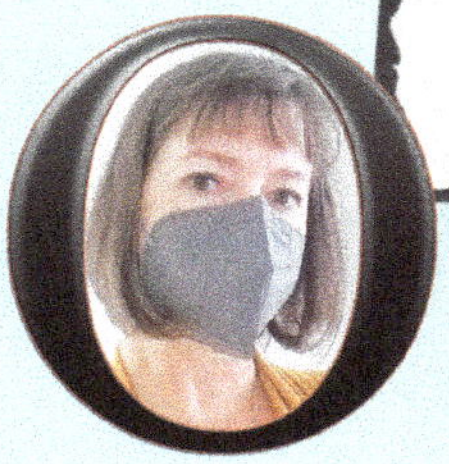

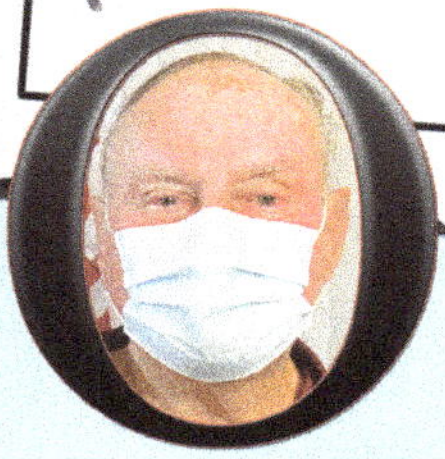

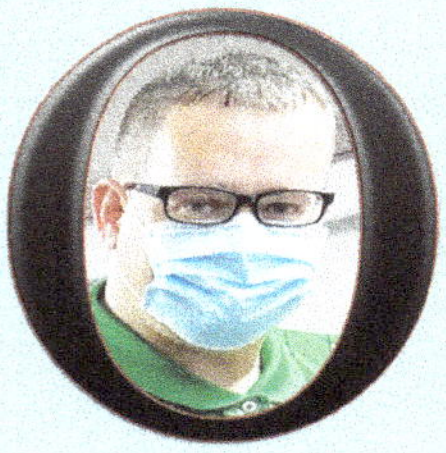

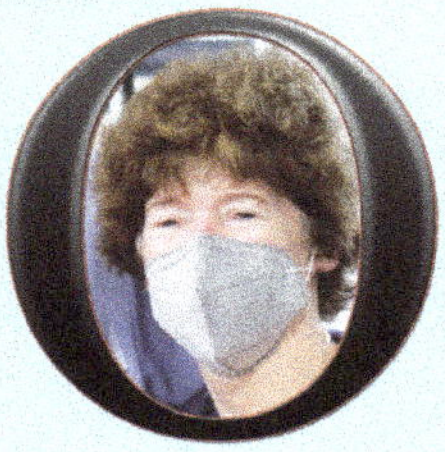

And yet we wear our masks
While in a public place,
Still others scream their freedom
To show their ugly face.

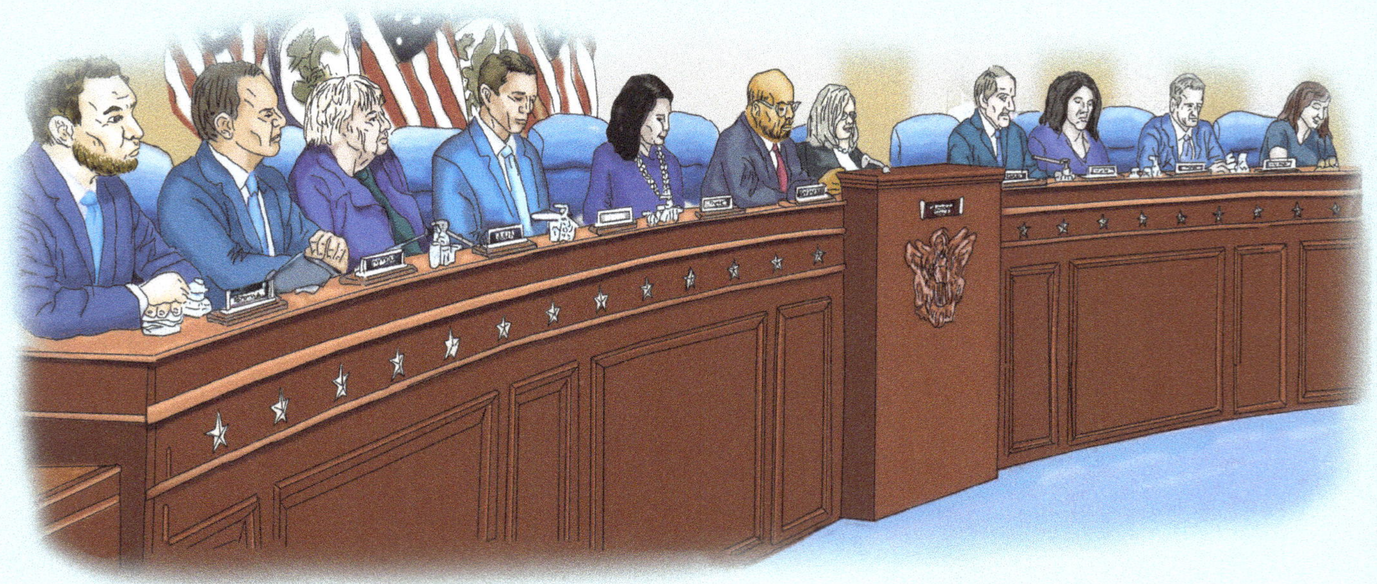

A January sixth
Committee formed to find
Who tried to overturn
What voters had consigned.

Our country now has changed.
The anger, hate, and lies
Have placed us in a spot
With weakened common ties.

In March a war began
By Russia in Ukraine,
Destroying, killing, taking;
Determined to regain.

A classroom in Uvalde,
As usual that day,
Sat learning lessons taught
With lunch not far away.

A person carried in
A weapon used for war,
To shoot those in the room
While cops watched by the door.

Then Covid Omicron
Attacked again in May
To overtake the others
And send them on their way.

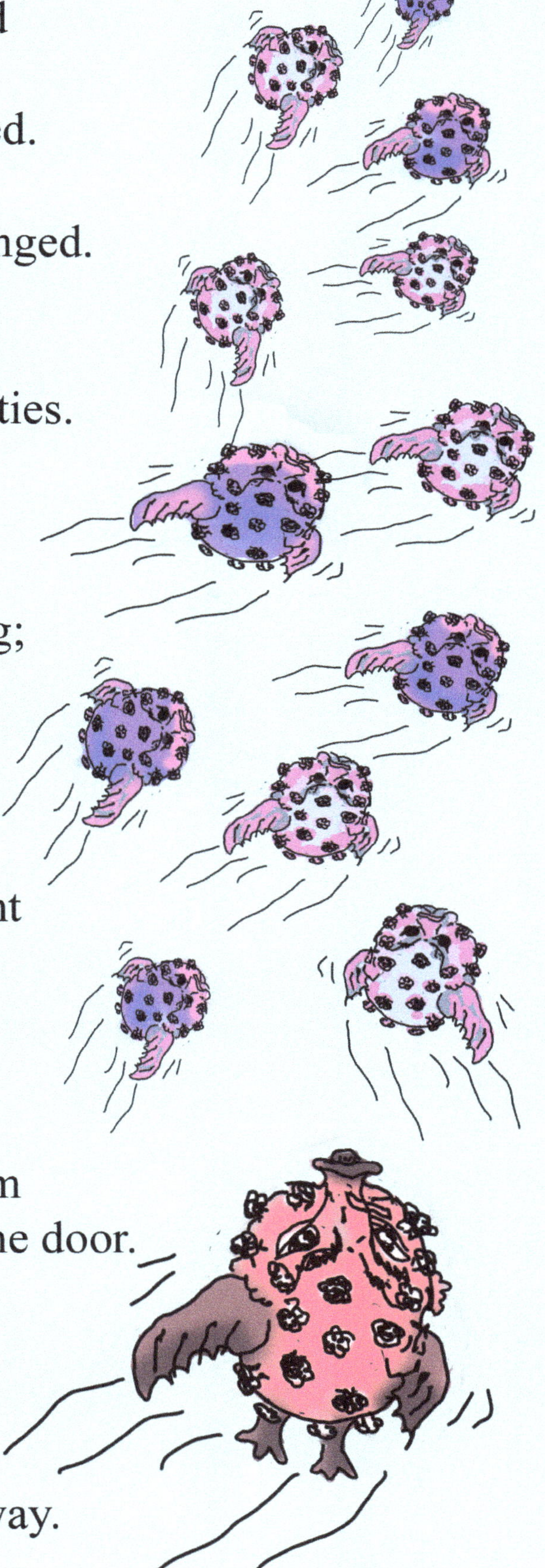

Our daughter came to visit
And do again our trip

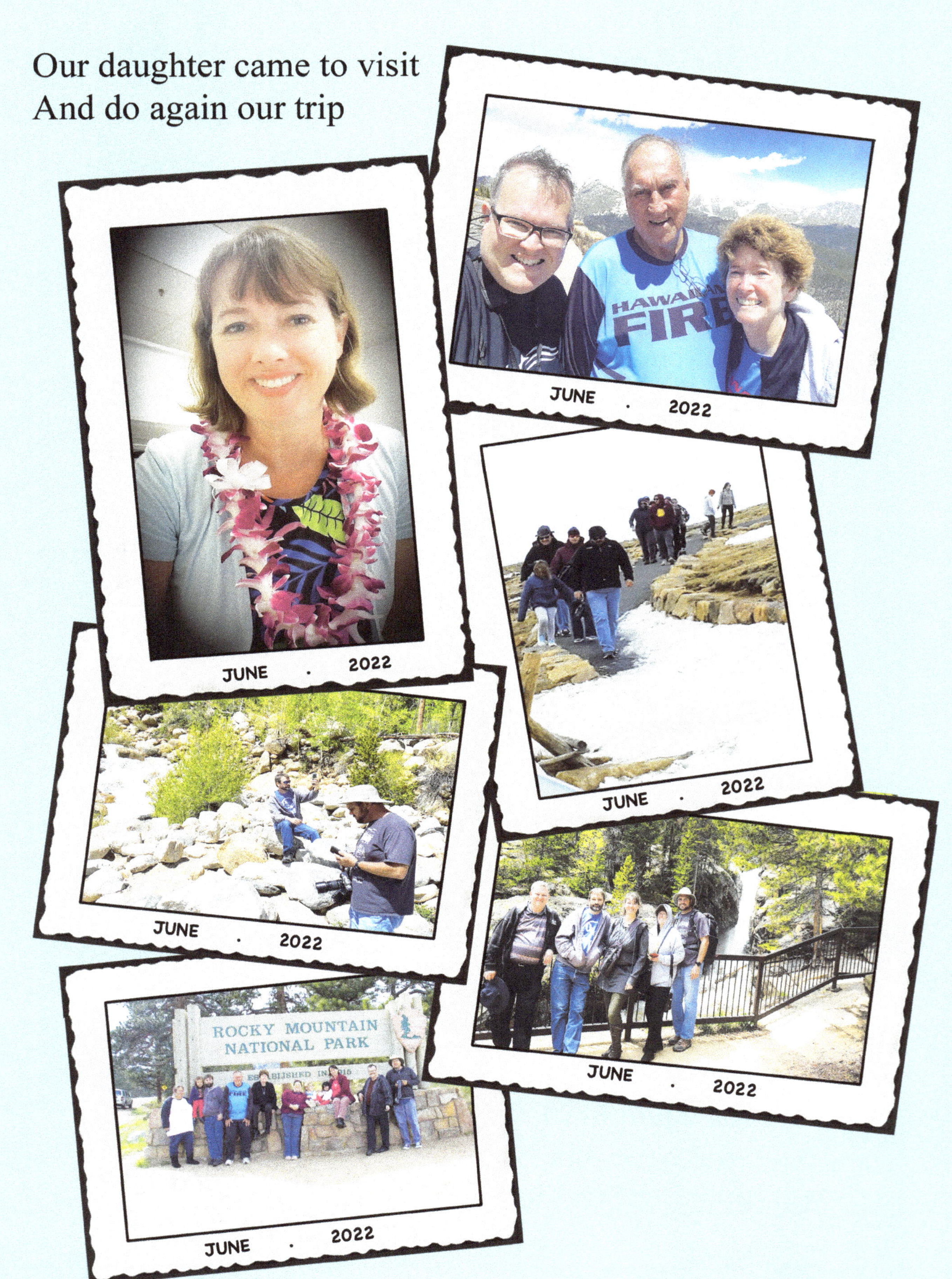

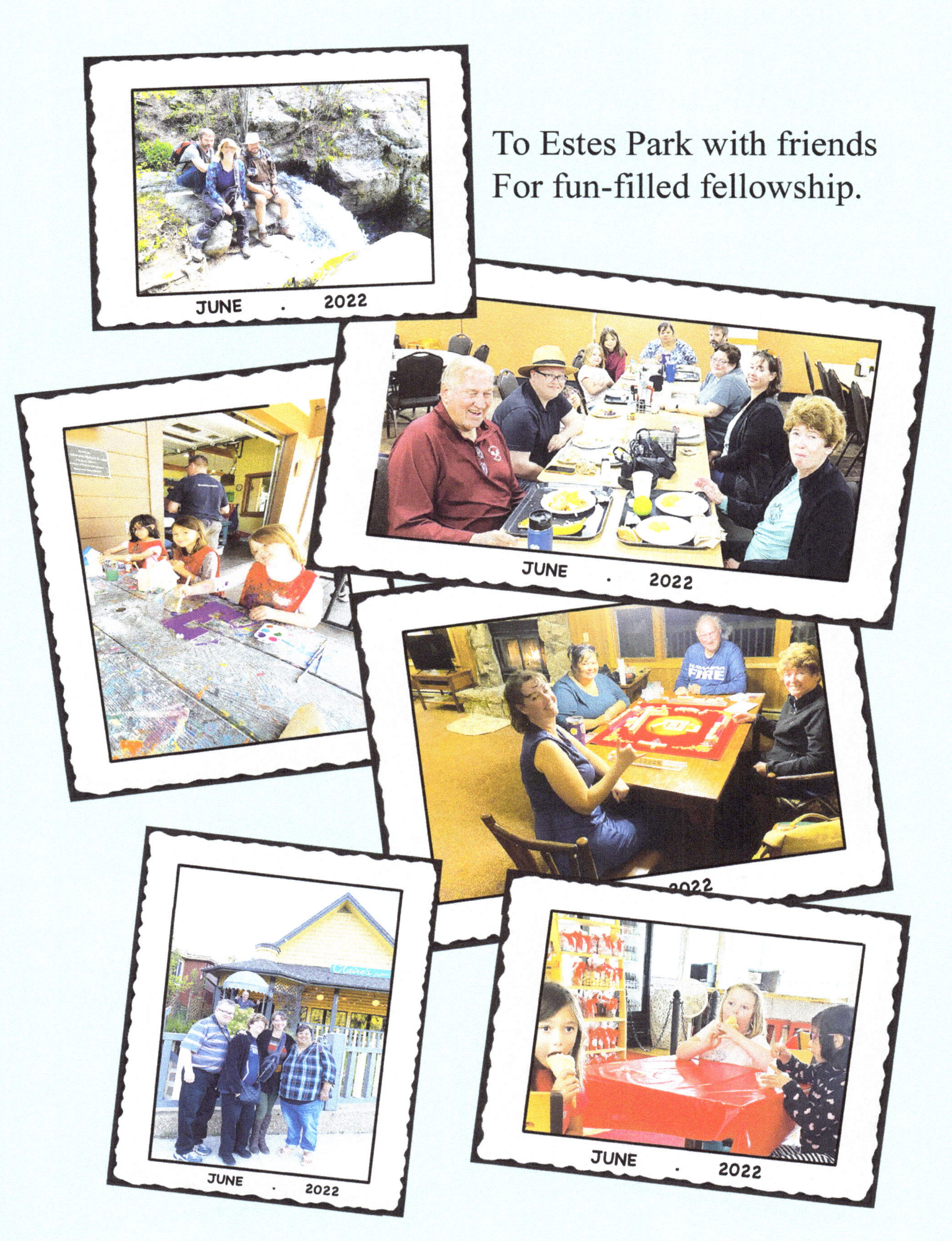

To Estes Park with friends
For fun-filled fellowship.

Our next trip turned toward Texas
To see our cousins there,
As well as, friends near them
Renewing ties we share.

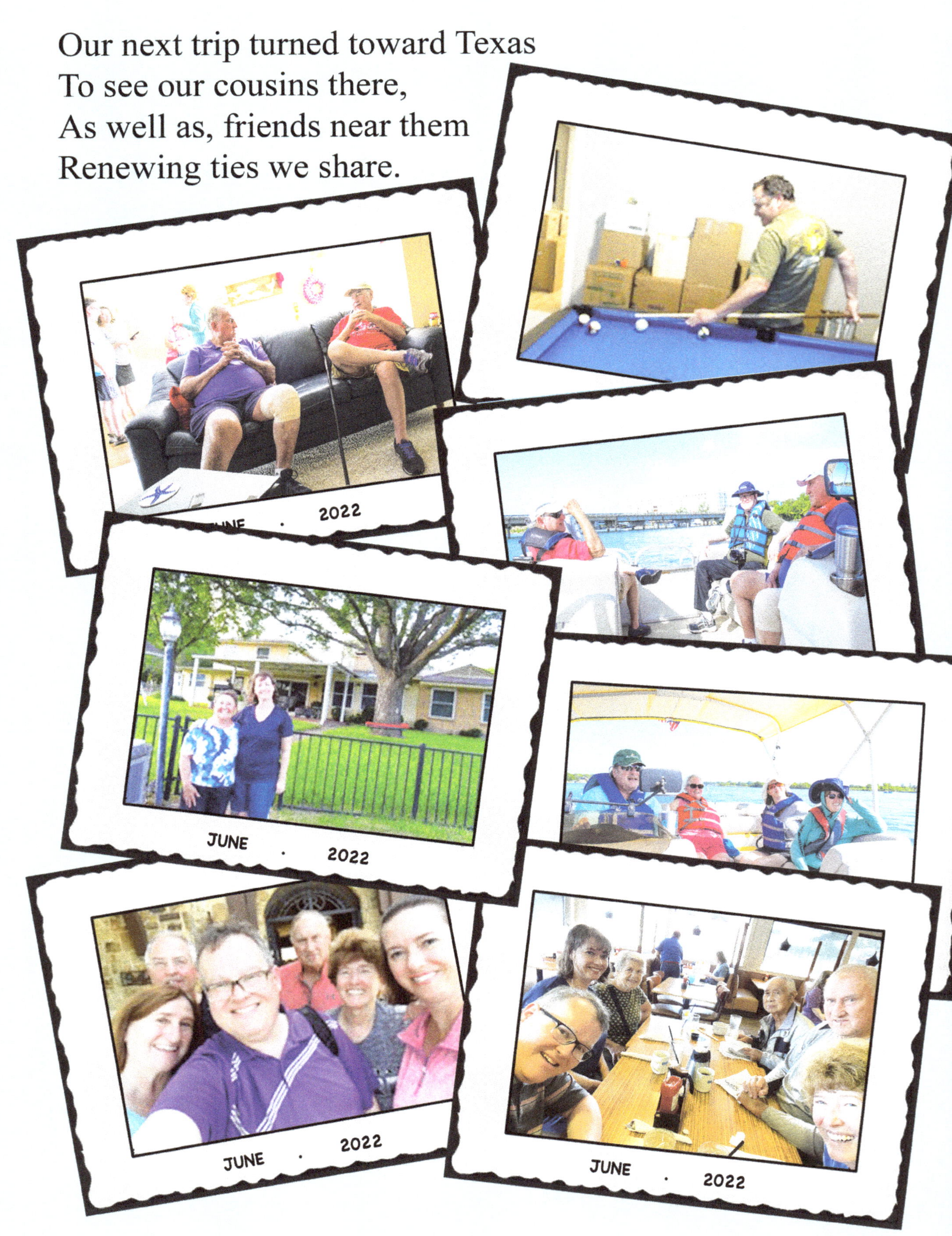

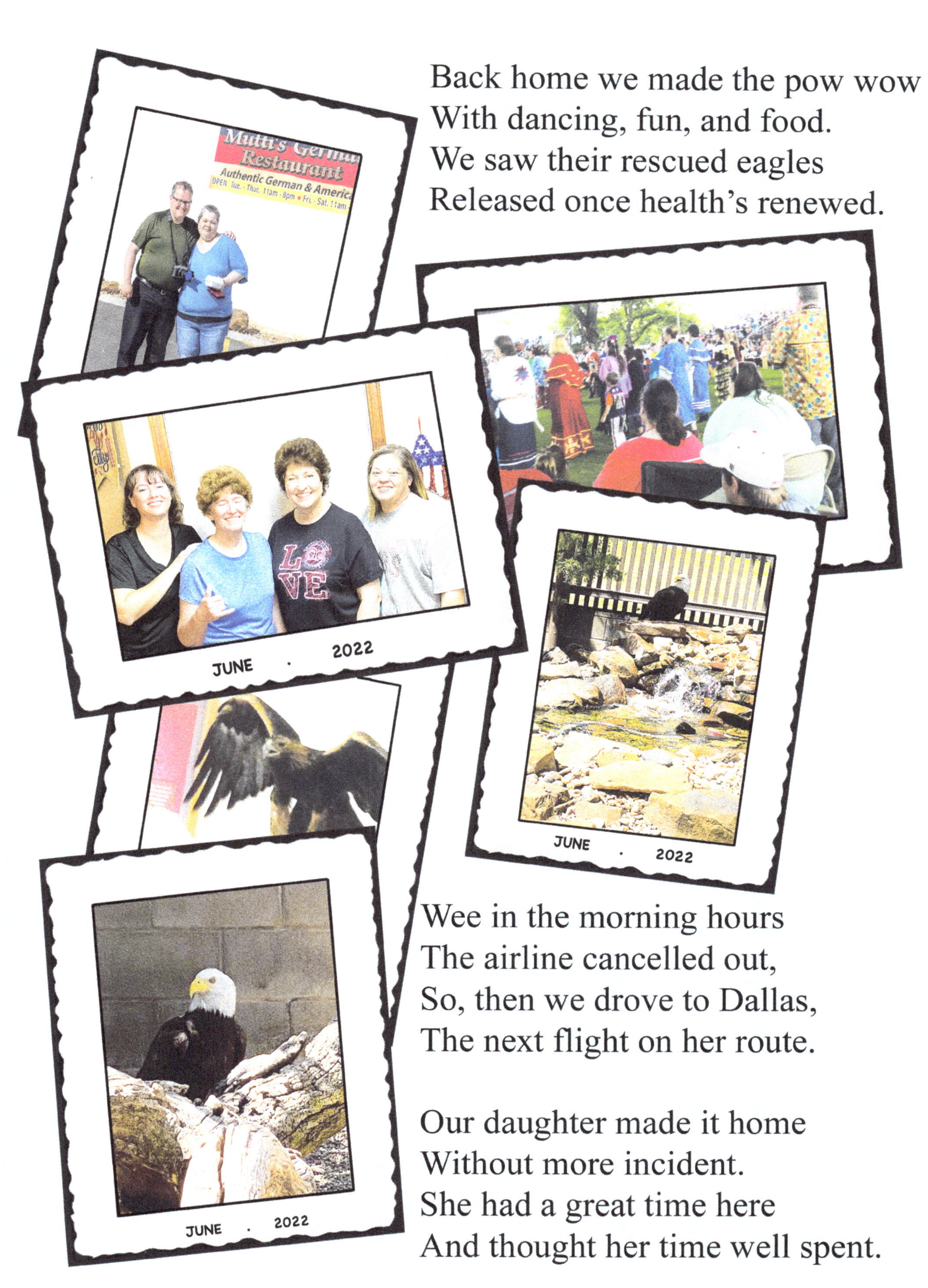

Back home we made the pow wow
With dancing, fun, and food.
We saw their rescued eagles
Released once health's renewed.

Wee in the morning hours
The airline cancelled out,
So, then we drove to Dallas,
The next flight on her route.

Our daughter made it home
Without more incident.
She had a great time here
And thought her time well spent.

My walking buddy suffered
A stroke two years ago.
It stopped our daily walks
That we enjoyed so.

This year on June the seventh,
My walking buddy passed.
She had recovered some,
But then declined so fast.

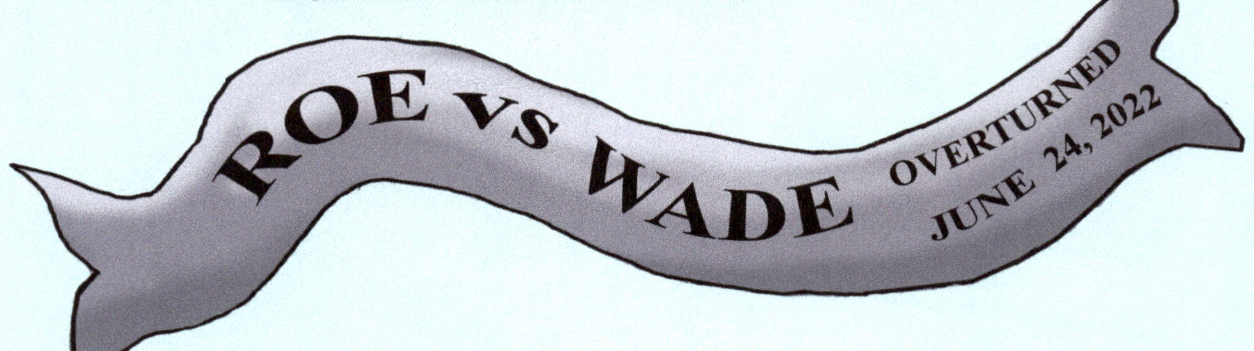

The twenty-fourth of June
Became a day for tears
For half the U.S. citizens
Lost freedoms theirs for years.

For on this day in June,
Six Justices replied,
"The precedence of Roe
And privacy denied."

They next attacked New York
Gun laws and called them void.
Amendment Number Two
Had rights to be enjoyed.

Court Justices also
Curtailed the EPA.
Oil companies could then
Resolve their own best way.

July the fourth we drove
To celebrate the day
And see some family
That lived some miles away.

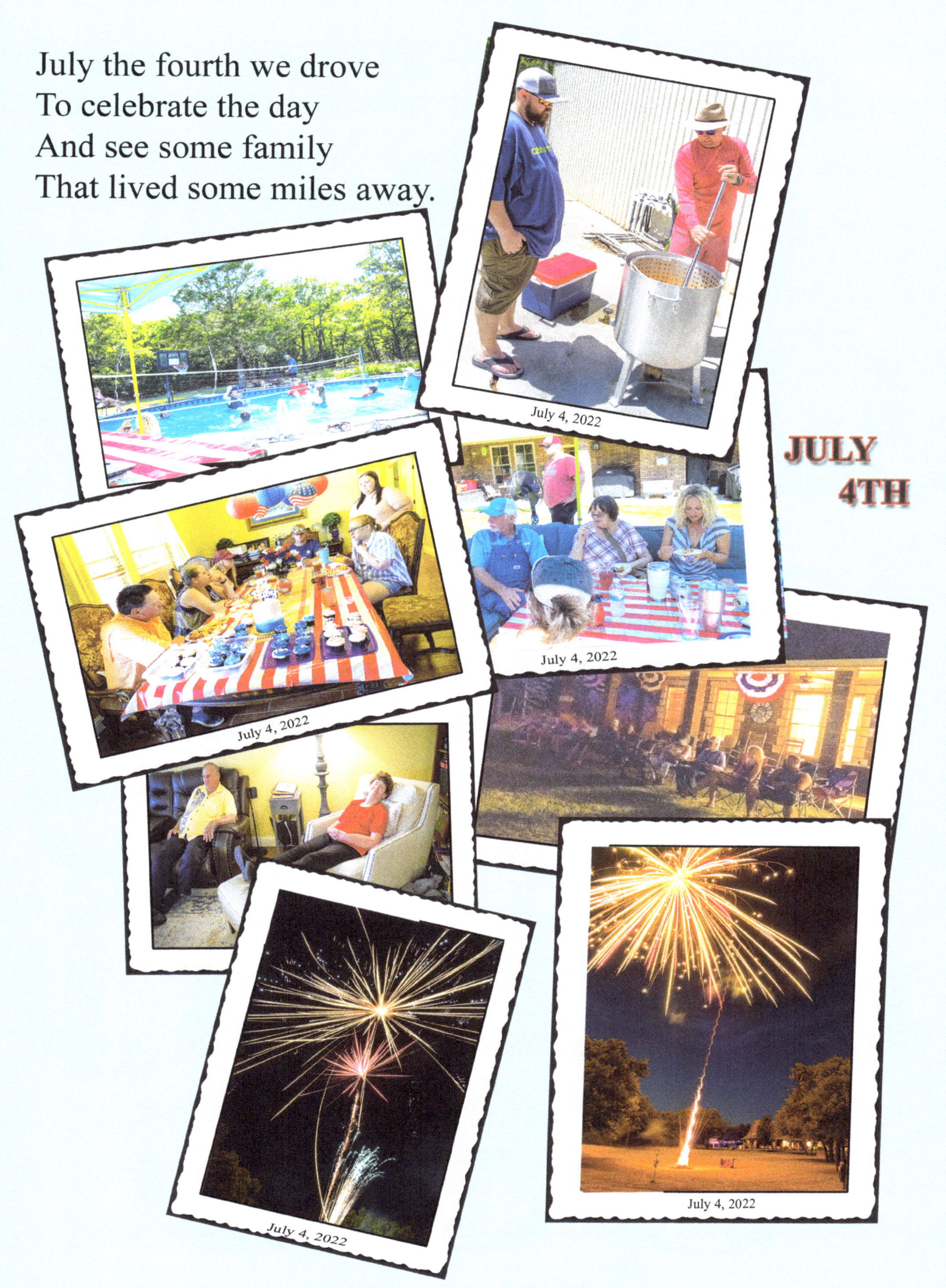

July 4, 2022

July 4, 2022

July 4, 2022

July 4, 2022

July 4, 2022

July 4, 2022

Then Congress passed a bill In Medicare and cutting
For things the nation sought Inflation rates somewhat.

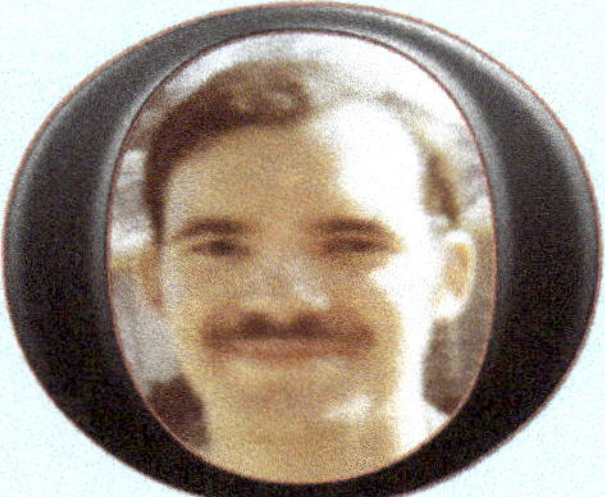 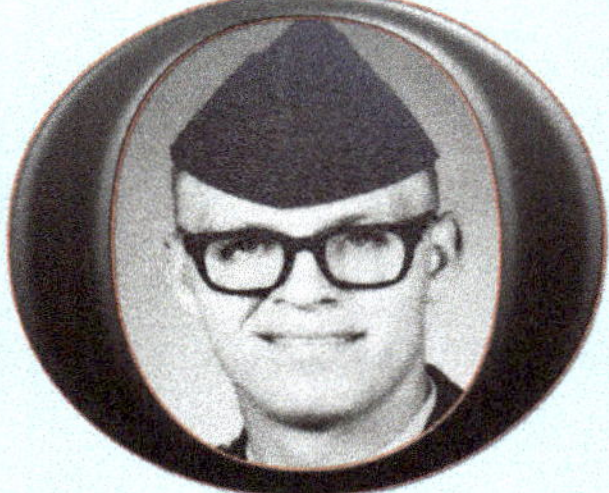 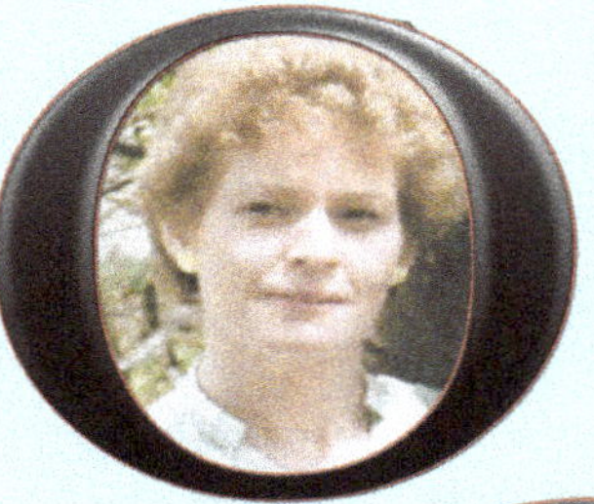

He planned our nine-eleven.
Two drones took out this man
Found after two decades
While in Afghanistan.

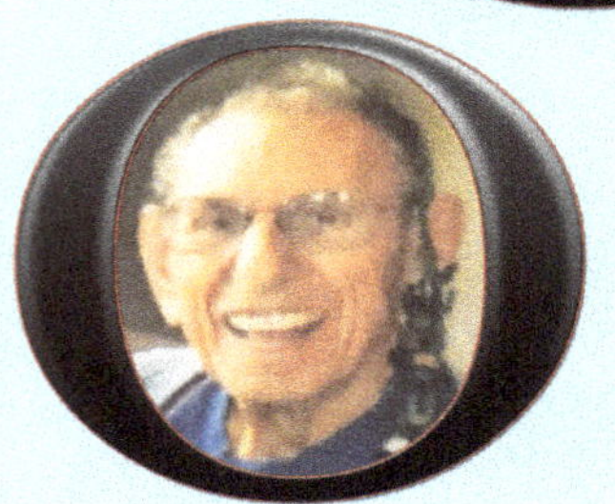 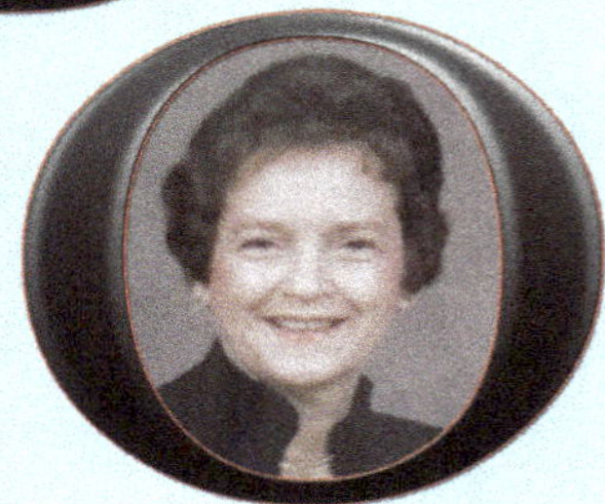

The Ukraine War by Russia
Caused price of gas to rise,
In food, our daily needs,
And most things otherwise.

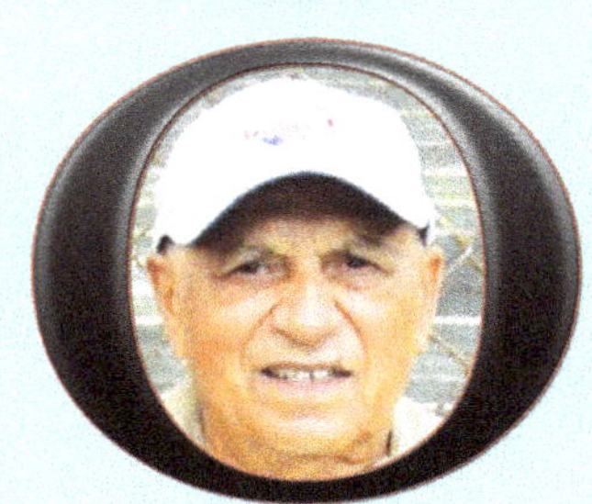 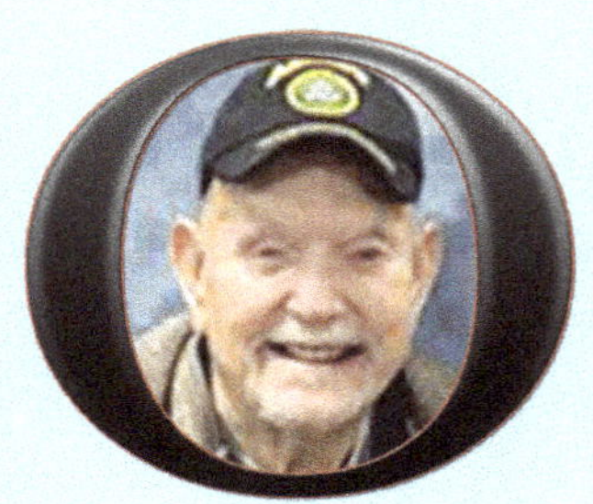

With new cars scarce to find,
Used cars sold just like new.
One party formed a cult
Refuting facts known true.

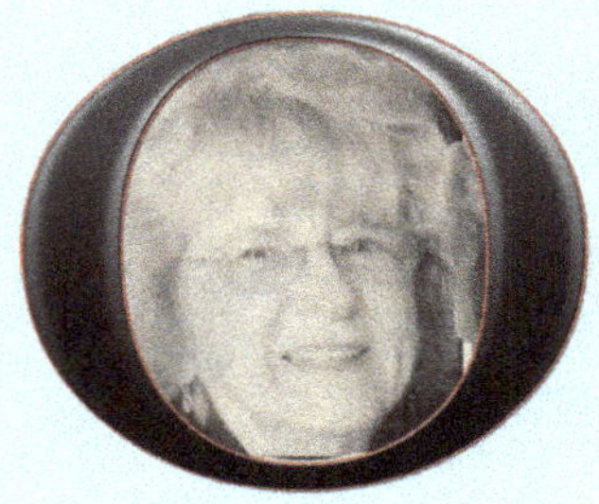 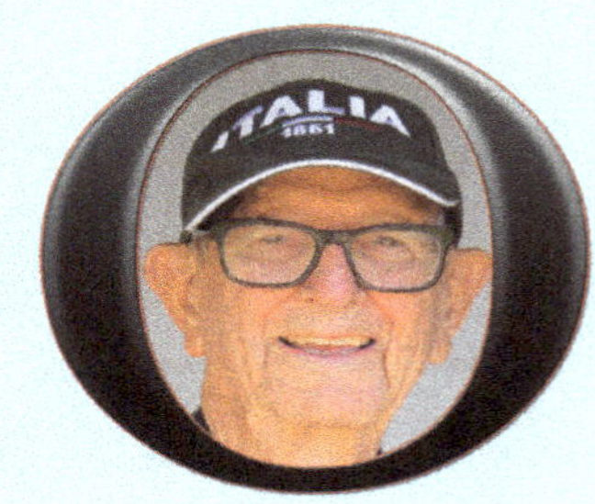

This span of daunting years
Caused loss of friends and kin
Though none succumbed to covid,
But other ills within.

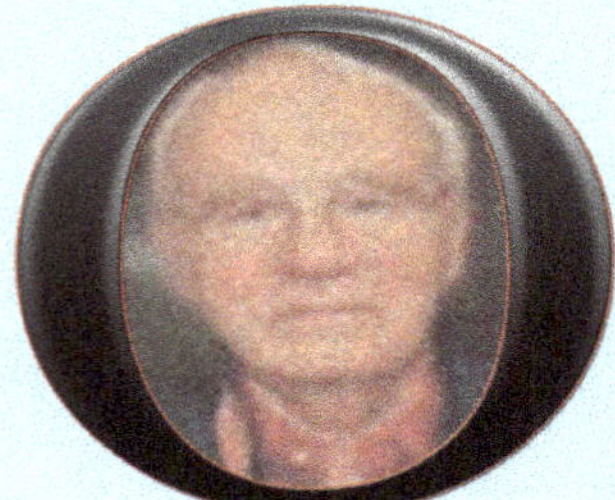 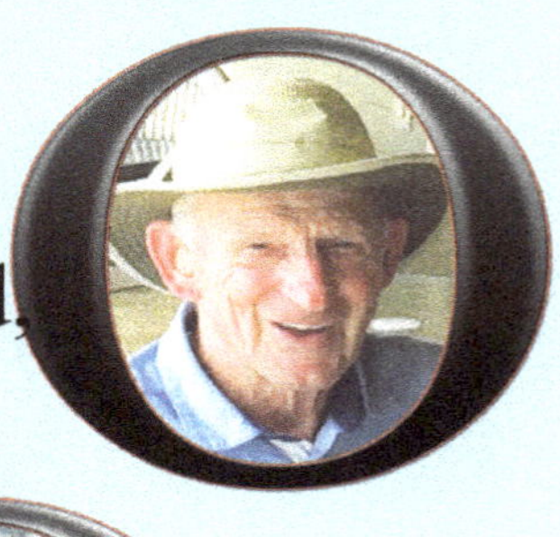

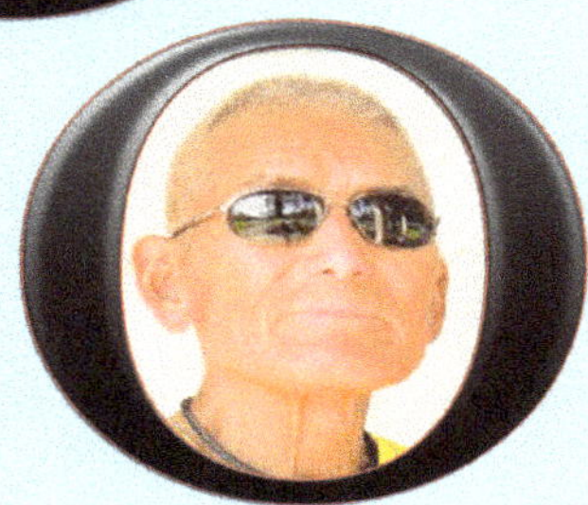 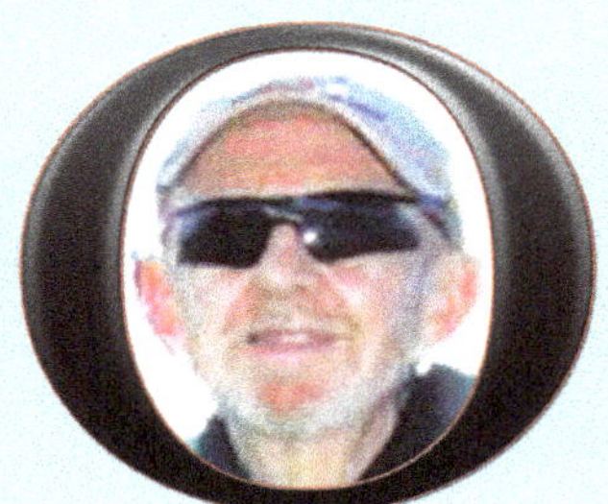 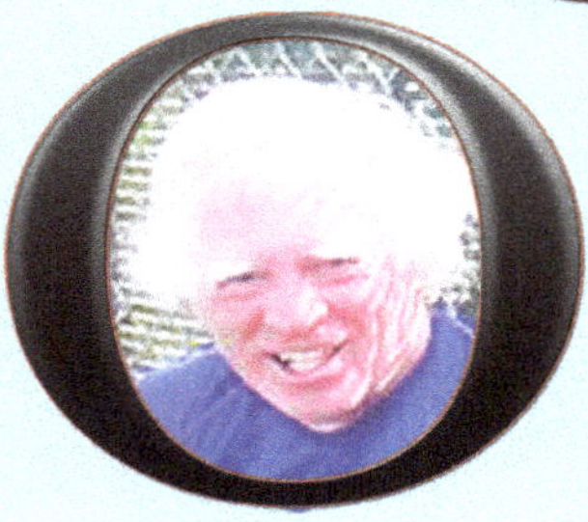

Although we stayed at home
While Covid stormed the land,
We flew in August to
Hawaii as we planned.

Our daughter picked us up
And took us to our place.
We settled in before
Resuming normal pace.

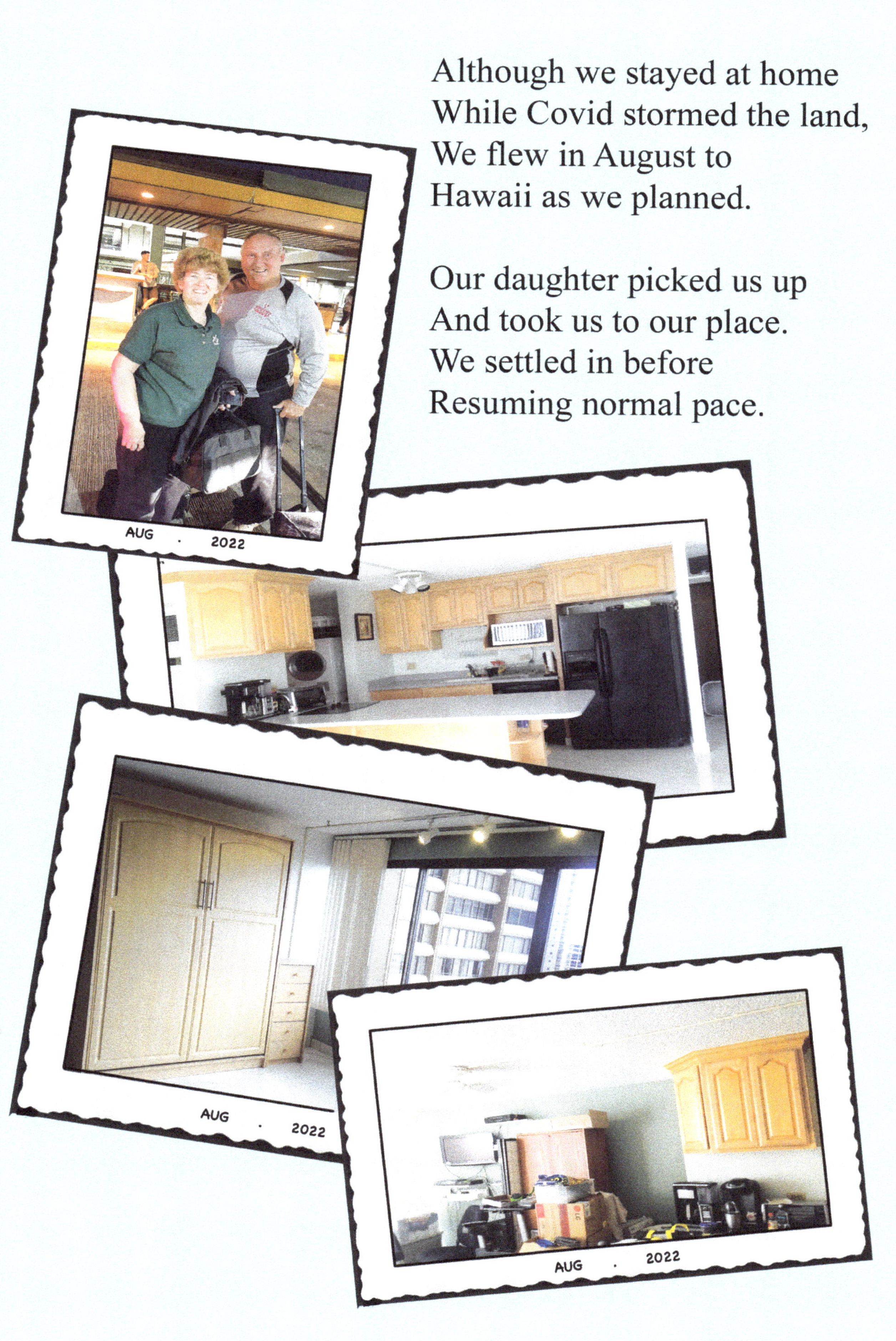

To reach the tennis courts,
We walked through Waikiki
To talk and watch the group
Play tennis skillfully.

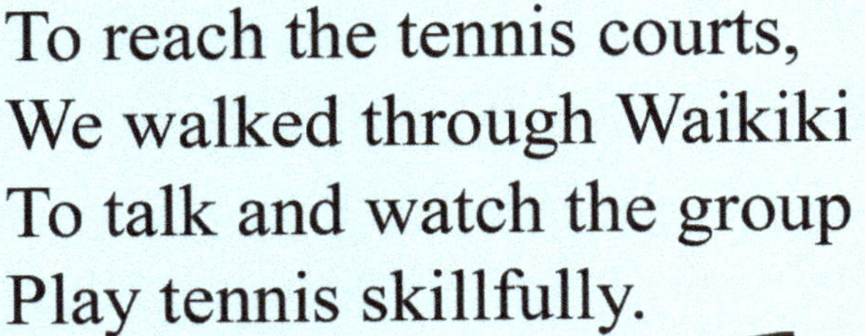

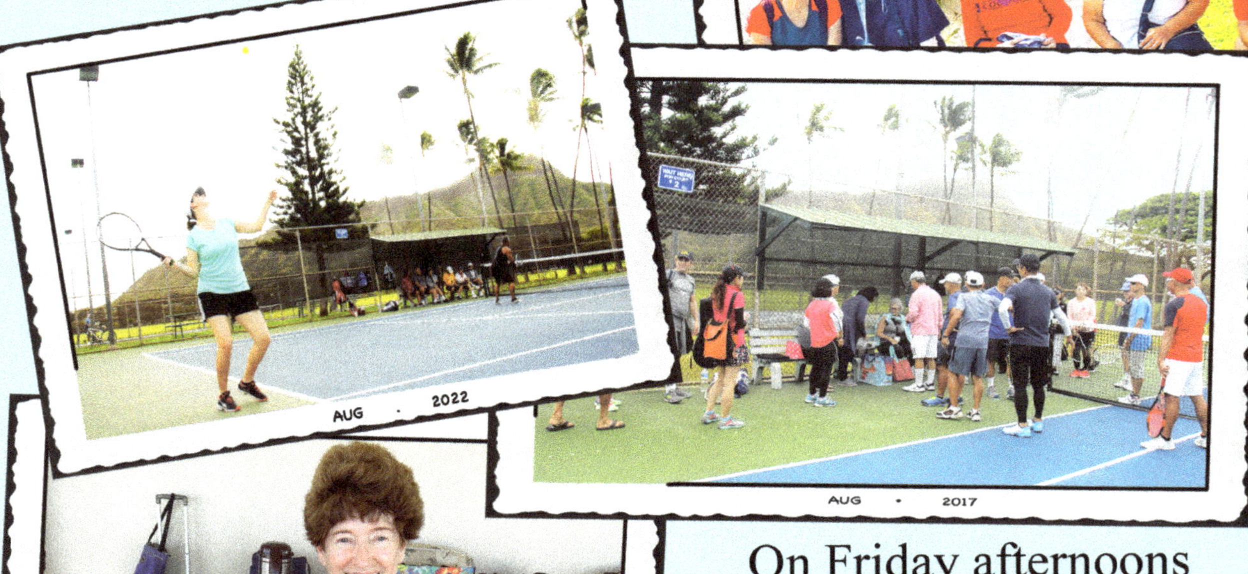

On Friday afternoons
We met with friends to play
Some Mahjong and enjoy
Their company that day.

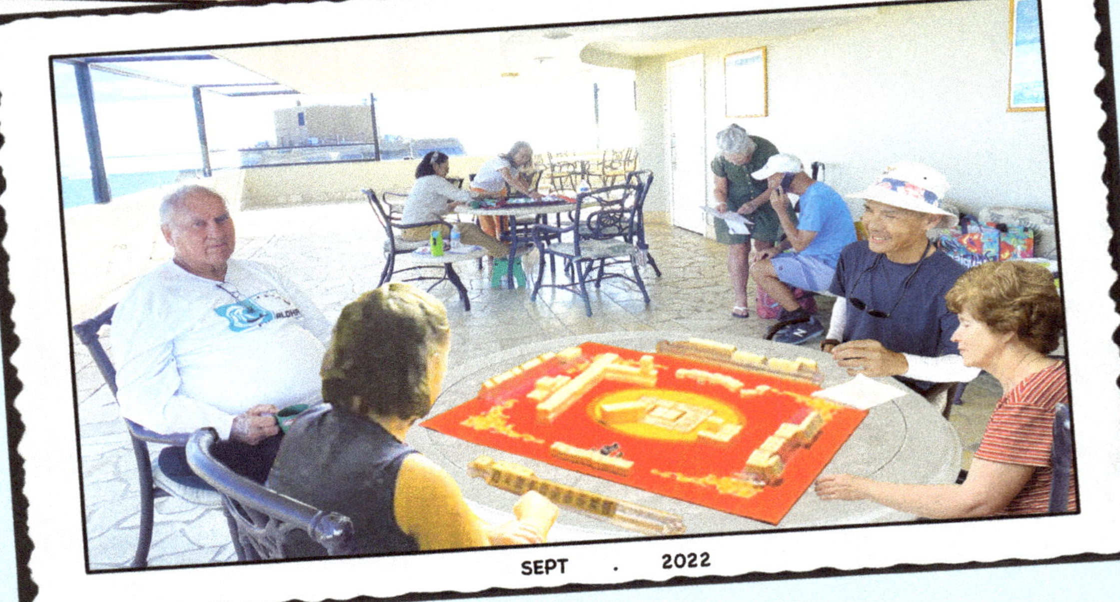

The harbor or the park,
Were places we would walk

With friends and family
To exercise and talk.

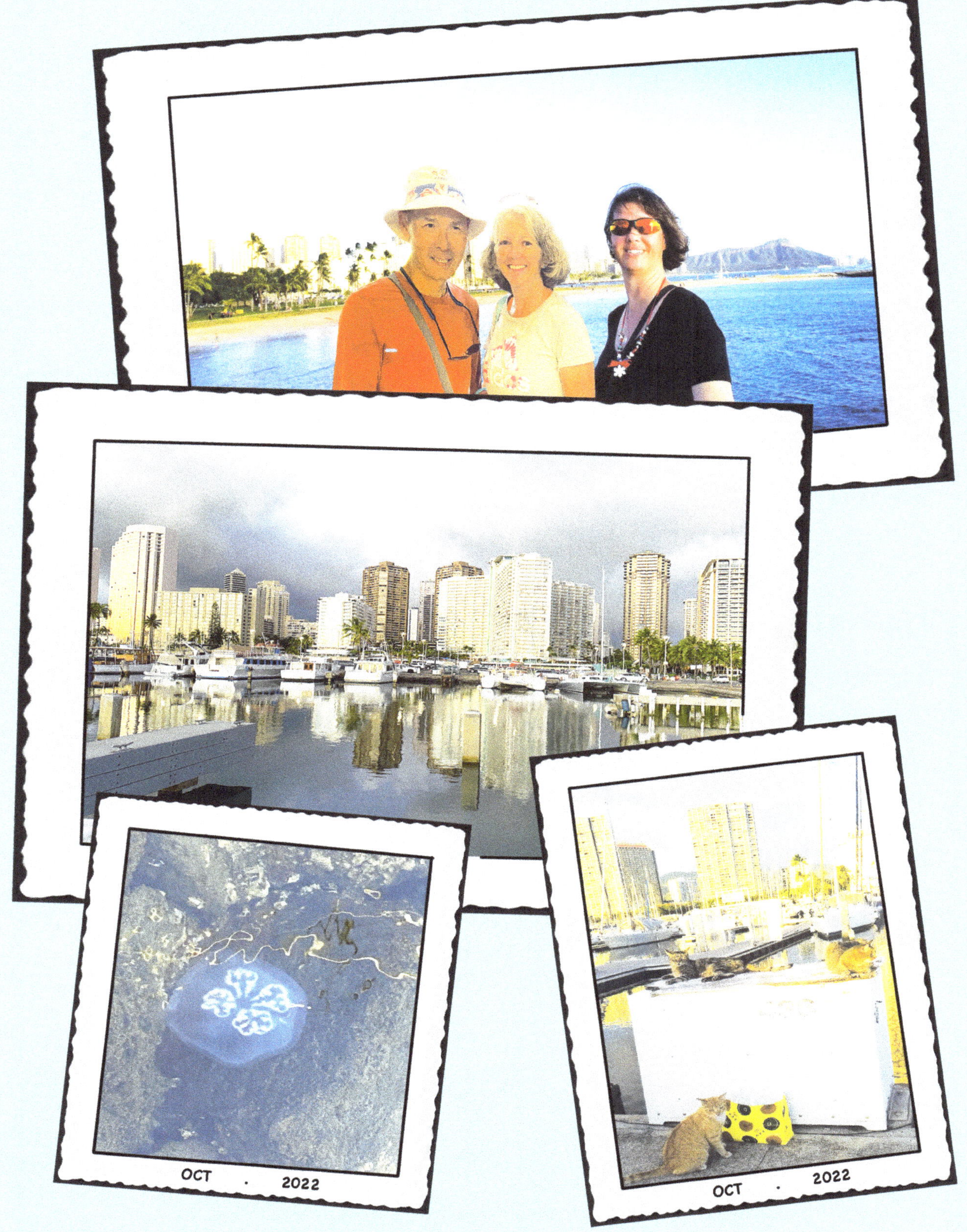

Election midterm came.
We voted as before.
The House lost democrats,
But kept their Senate core.

The last few months a threat
Now ravages our land
With Covid, RSV,
And flu germs close at hand.

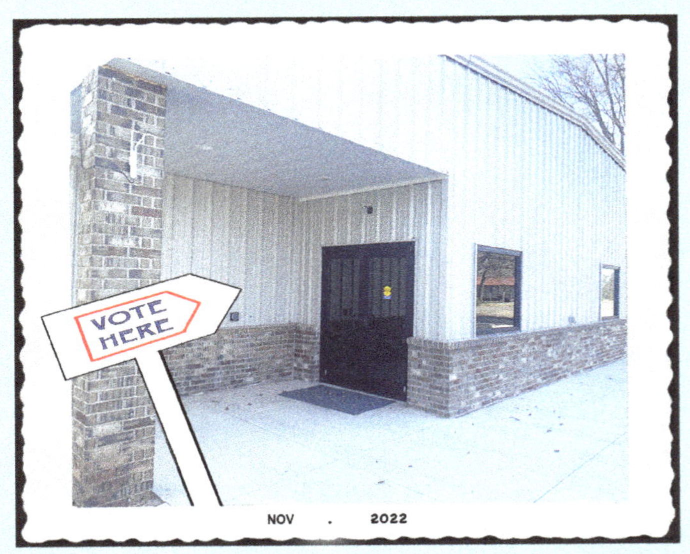

Somehow, we caught the Covid
With symptoms as to note:
A runny nose, a temp,
A cough, and painful throat.

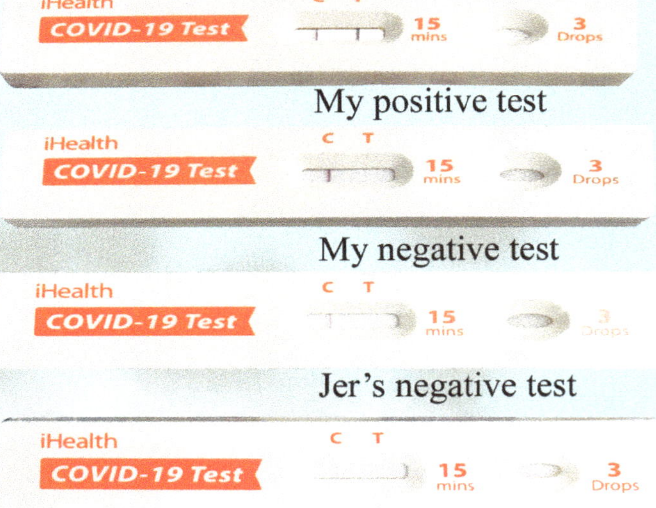

My positive test

My negative test

Jer's negative test

Johnny's negative test

Then Mauna Loa once
Again began to pour
Its lava out in rivers
As it had done before.

Next Kilauea joined
To spout its lava too,
But soon they both cooled down
To cease their fiery spew.

A Special Council then,
To search out facts and who
Had done the wrongful things,
Subpoenaed those who knew.

With this the former one
Began to whine and vent
For Constitution termination
And be returned as president.

An Arctic blast burst down
To bring some winter woe
With winds that fiercely blew
The freezing rain and snow.

The day of Winter Solstice
Some Council facts came out.
Our daughter flew to Dallas
With zero cold about.

Our cousin picked her up.
We drove to meet her there
And saw our friends and cousins
With season's joy to share.

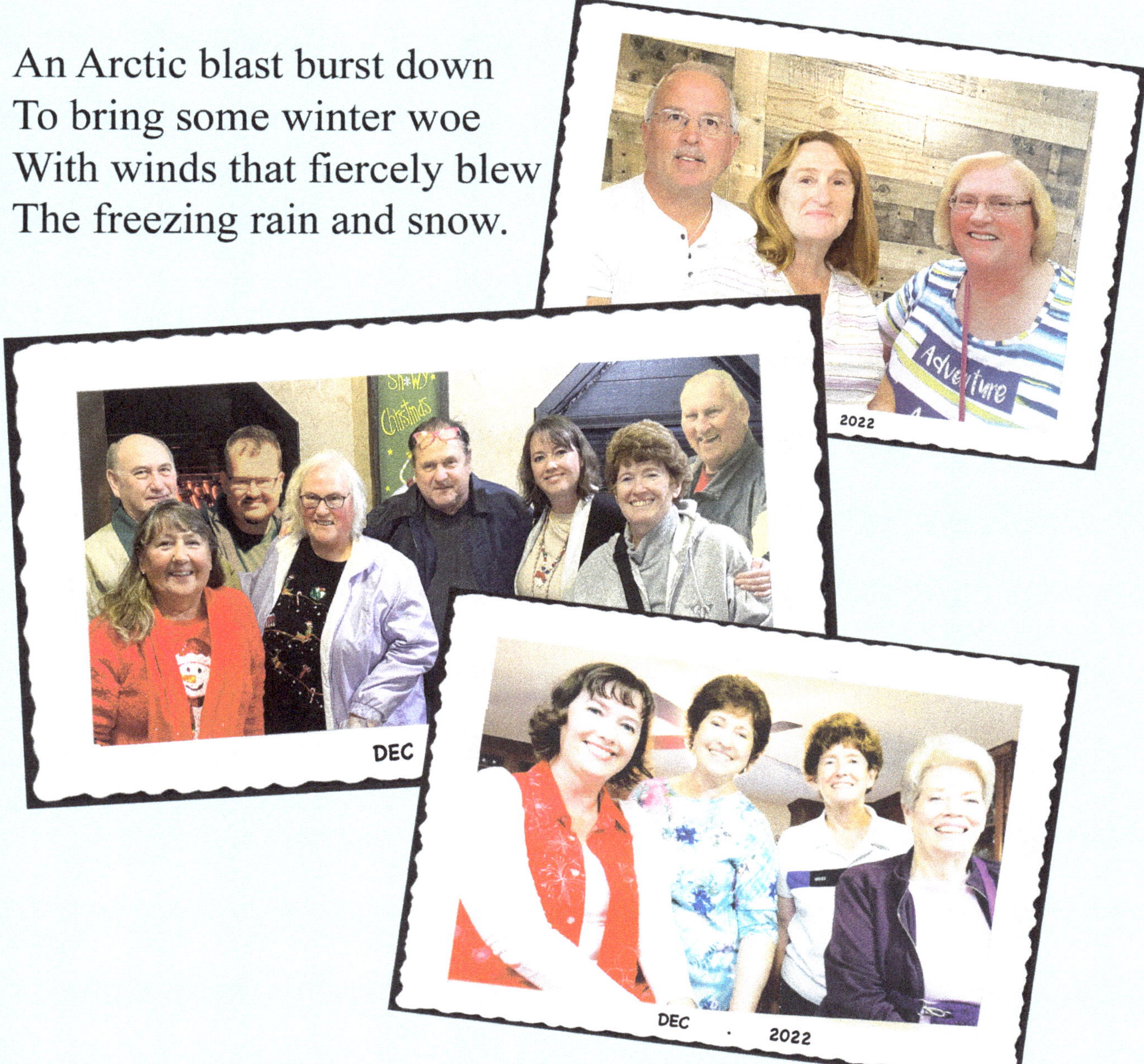

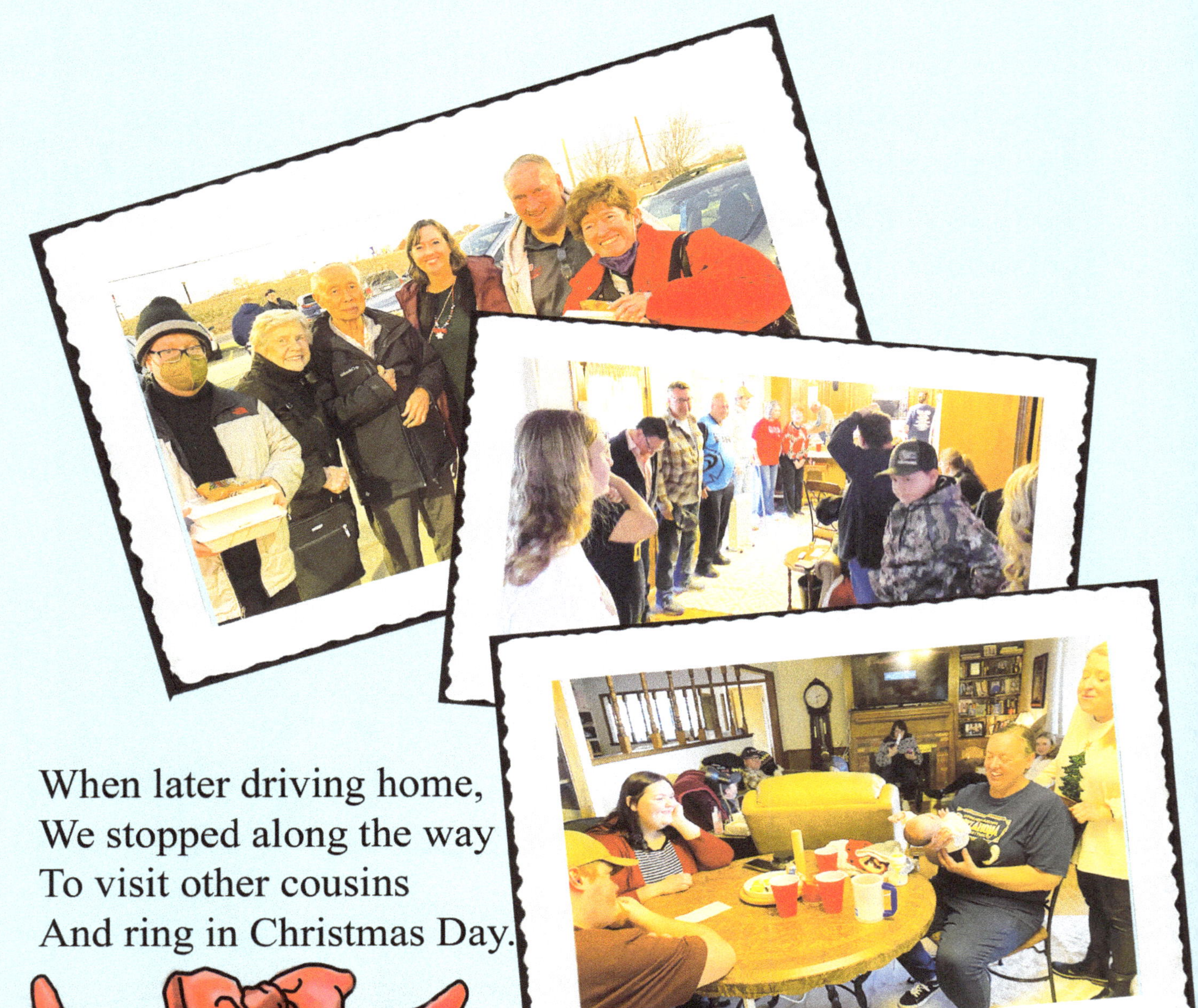

When later driving home,
We stopped along the way
To visit other cousins
And ring in Christmas Day.

The Ukraine President
Zelensky flew to see
Our President and Congress
For some diplomacy.

He talked about their struggle
To keep their sovereignty,
Their thankfulness for help,
And for democracy.

The Arctic blast brought weather
That cancelled many flights
And left some thousands stranded
From reaching destined sites.

The old year passed away
With bravo as it passed.
We did not mourn its passing
But hailed its close at last.

JANUARY 2023

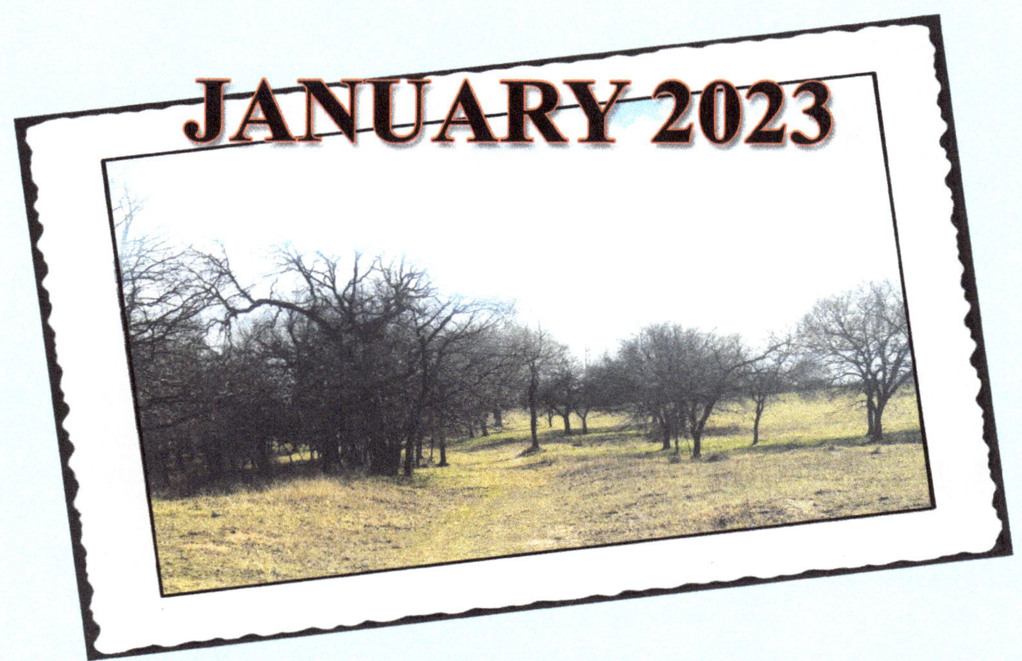

The New Year's Day came in
With clouds but weather clear,
A better way to start
This first day of the year.

His long State of the Union
Addressed the things he'd done
And what he hoped to do
With all in unison.

Since all of this began,
We've always lived with hope.
Though sometimes trapped in strife,
We still have learned to cope.

We do not know our future,
But we must carry through
And make each day our best
In all we say and do.

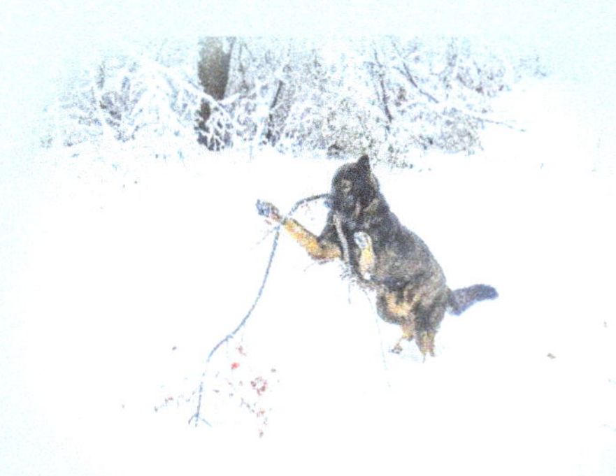

Alice: *"Oh, I forgot to put a dollar under her pillow!"*
Jon: *"Here. Put it under there before she wakes up."*
As she placed the dollar under the pillow, Allie woke up.
Allie: *"Are you the tooth fairy?"*
Alice: *"Yes, but don't tell Ellie."*
Allie: *"Ok, but you need to give me another dollar!"*

Jeremy's FB entry: We ordered Vienna Sausages from Sam's online and the app insisted on mailing it. We made sure of the address since Jami uses the same Sam's account. Guess who got the Vienna sausages today?

Jami's Account: "Dad, Mel just called me and said you have a package from Sam's! Then he asked when you got in! I told him you were still in Oklahoma."
Dad: "Well, we were expecting a case of Vienna Sausages! Looks like you are set for hurricane season! The vienna sausages missed us by 4200 miles TO END UP IN HAWAII!"

We were expecting a package from our daughter. Eventually she called saying it had been delivered. We looked. No package. We checked everywhere at least twice. Finally, we texted her that no package had been delivered. She called the delivery company. Their records showed it had been delivered; however, they had no photo showing it, but it had been delivered to the correct place. If not found in a couple of days, they would refund her money. Once our son got home from work that night, he told us the delivery truck arrived just as he reached our driveway that morning. He received the package and put it in his trunk for safe keeping and then forgot about it. We called our daughter. She called the delivery company to apologize for her misinformation.

When our propane tank gets down to 30%, our supplier comes out to fill our tank. Johnny had gone out to talk to him. The German Shepherd dog next door, Pluto, heard them talking and ran as rapidly as he could toward them. The man filling our tank looked very worried. Johnny said, "Don't worry. He's just wanting to play ball."
At that exact moment, Pluto stopped at the man's feet and dropped his ball!

After the last ice storm, Johnny drove his lawn mower around the yard picking up fallen limbs and sticks. He either dragged them to the burn pile or placed them in the mower's trailer. Pluto saw him in the yard, crawled under the fence, and joined in what he took to be a game. Grabbing onto the ends of the sticks he helped pull. Once they were delivered to the burn pile, Pluto picked one up in his mouth, and ran with it to wherever Johnny happened to be at the moment. He had a great game going of playing fetch.

Johnny worked mulching the fallen leaves. Among the leaves he found and picked up pine cones. I helped him pick them up and place them in a plastic trashbag. He had gotten back on the mower to do more leaf mulching when Pluto came over to help us. We played some fetch with him, so he ran after whatever we tossed to retrieve and bring it back to us. Finally he caught sight of the trashbag of pine cones which we had placed away from where Johnny mulched. He dearly loved playing with the pine cones. The next thing we knew, Pluto had grabbed the bag and ran for home. I guess that's one way to clear the yard of pine cones!

www.ingramcontent.com/pod-product-compliance
Lightning Source LLC
Chambersburg PA
CBHW040858070726
47599CB00035B/2035